The ECONOMIC GOSPEL FOR THE USA IS HERE!!!

WINNING THE GREAT WIN-WIN
FOR AMERICA AND THE WORLD

Carlton Buford

The Economic Gospel for the USA is Here!!!

Cover design & Typeset in Garamond Pro by riverdesignbooks.com

ISBN 979-8-218-52198-1 (Print)
ISBN 979-8-218-52199-8 (Ebook)

CONTENTS

INTRODUCTION

The Economic Gospel for the USA is the good news for the United States of America and the rest of the world of how America can and will lead at home and globally in ways that will unify America and the citizens of the world to willfully and synergistically work together to win the "Great Win-Win" for all of humanity on this planet!

What is the win-win, you ask?

We create and sustain the "best" opportunities for all the nations of the world and all the individuals within all the nations of the world to be the "best" versions of themselves possible in the same way that we love, care for, protect, and treat our own children.

This is the secret sauce to successful life and prosperity for all humankind. The Economic Gospel for the USA heals both the exploiters and the exploited—individually, as families, communities, states, nations, and the entire world.

In concept, the Economic Gospel for the USA is nothing new. It's about Americans falling in love with being Americans and showing that love by being American to other Americans and being Americans to the rest of the world. *That* is the solution. *That* is the Great Win-Win that the world so desperately needs: Americans falling in love with who we are again and simply being the best versions of who we naturally are to other Americans and to other people in the world.

But there is so much division, hatred, and strife both in America and around the world. So how in the world can this book help us save ourselves from ourselves?

Who are Americans? What defines an American, and what will help Americans fall in love with and be proud to be American once more? The US Constitution is the document that all Americans pledge their allegiance to, and it's this document that we should look to first for what it means to be an American.

The Preamble to the Constitution lays out beautifully who Americans are:

> "We, the People of the United States, in Order to form a more perfect Union, establish Justice, insure domestic Tranquility, provide for the common defense, promote the general Welfare, and secure the Blessings of Liberty to ourselves and our Posterity, do ordain and establish this Constitution for the United States of America."

The Preamble is an introduction, purpose, and strategic planning document that describes what America is and who we are, and strategically, how we should go about being who we say we are to ourselves, to each other, and to others outside our country.

America is the only country on the planet where the people are in charge of themselves, the government, and all the rules that dictate economics, public policy, and international affairs—all activities and pursuits related to life, education, career, entertainment, culture, and so on.

Americans are exemplified by the phrase "We, the People of the United States, in order to form a more perfect Union . . ." This statement implies that when Americans are deciding about how they will live, study, work, and play together, they will make the time, effort, and investments necessary to consider and include all the people of the United States of America in the decision-making process so that, to the greatest extent possible, the decisions made about how we work, study, play and live together give everyone in America the opportunity to become the best version of themselves possible.

The US Constitution is a wonderful document. It is very considerate of Americans' rights and beliefs, both as individuals and as collective citizens of the United States of America. The issue with America historically and to this day is not with the Constitution but with Americans who only want to follow it and work with their fellow Americans when the Constitution works expressly in their favor or to the detriment or destruction of those they disagree with or oppose.

Disagreements or even 180-degree opposite views are not unproductive or undesirable in a democracy. Differences and opposing views are signposts in a democracy showing that there are opportunities to learn from our differences in ways that create and maintain new and better solutions or alternative ways of thinking about doing things, which accommodate and make life much better for all.

Differences looked upon as problems or fatal flaws in the group with the differing view are not in line with the ideals of democracy. They are rather reflective of laziness and disrespect for the lives and values of others because we do not want to make the time to learn and discover how our differences can create solutions and value added that may exceed our wildest expectations. Autocratic and authoritarian governments or societies have no patience with or empathy for difference, diversity, or inclusion. As a democracy, we should be different.

Democracy builds and strengthens a nation's ability to adapt and thrive in an environment that is constantly evolving and changing unexpectedly. Effective democracies embrace change as a constant and use that change and the diversity in their population as fuel and feedstock to create synergies and productivity in the economy and society.

The essential challenge from the beginning of human civilization has been whether humankind will choose to develop or "exploit" one another while living, working, learning, and playing together on this planet. The problem is that much more effort, creativity, patience, empathy, perseverance, hard work, and leadership are required to develop than to exploit—but the benefit of all that effort is the "Great Win-win" solution for everyone.

Making time to consider the idiosyncrasies of individuals while maximizing the miraculous, almost inconceivable productivities created from the collective synergy that is produced from strategically aligning and integrating the vast diversity of talents and resources inherent in our nation is essential if we are to succeed in creating a fairer, more considerate, inclusive and respectful planet.

Economics and morality are inseparable. You cannot properly do one without the other. However, exploitative behavior teaches us that some regard morality and economics as completely separate and independent concepts and disciplines. Exploitative behavior always starts with the fundamental belief that the Great Win-win is absolutely impossible and unachievable, not because they have absolute proof and actual evidence that the Great Win-win is unachievable but because they do not want to put in the hard work and effort required to do the right thing.

Exploiters do not want to compete on a level playing field and do not want to have to put in the time and ingenuity required to figure out how to compete and take part in a way that allows them to win and still creates enough value that their efforts allow others with whom they work, compete, and play to also have the best opportunity to win.

Exploitation is always the quickest and easiest way for the exploiting group of people to win at catastrophically excessive levels, on the backs of, or at the expense or even the destruction of, the people being exploited.

Exploiters are always lying and distorting reality, truth, and history to justify their immoral and destructive behavior against the exploited so that they can continue their exploitation both now and in the future or so that they can keep what they have gained through their exploitation. Exploitative behavior always creates a justification for separating or breaking apart the "We" or "All" into the "Us" vs. "Them," where the "Good People" or the "Justified People" or the chosen "Us" are always better than or superior to the "Them" or "Others."

Now, I'm going to blow your mind.

Exploiters are not just the rich and powerful who use their power to trick, manipulate, lie, steal, bully, or kill others to get what they want by persuasion or force, whichever is required to get what they want. Exploiters can also be the poor and the weak, who use their vulnerable conditions to make themselves victims and lie, steal, cheat, kill, and create chaos to get sympathy from the public, the government, or anyone or any group in power to get what they want, at the expense or even destruction of others.

There are countless thousands and millions of examples of exploitation in the human experience. I will grab one recent and very memorable example from American history.

Between 2020 and 2021, in less than two years, more Americans were unjustly and needlessly killed by Covid-19 than all the American soldiers killed in all American wars since the Civil War until today. Can you fathom that? In just two years, more Americans were unjustly and unnecessarily killed by Covid-19 than all the soldiers who fought and were killed in all American wars from the Civil War of the 1860s to today.

Prior to Covid-19, could anyone have ever imagined that a country as wealthy, powerful, sophisticated, and medically equipped as the United States of America would ever have experienced the absolute worst and by far the highest death count associated with Covid-19, compared to any other country on the planet? How or why was this even remotely possible?

The Republican Party, led by the President of the United States, used the Covid-19 pandemic as an opportunity to exploit and divide the American people to gain and maintain political power, influence, and wealth leading up to the 2020 presidential election. To do this, former President Donald Trump purposely played down the seriousness and known remedies for protecting the American public from Covid-19. He told America and his supporters over the course of 2020, almost right up to election day, that Covid-19 was no worse than the common cold and that it would just go away on its own. He said there was no need to worry, fret, or do anything drastic, even after seeing hundreds of thousands of Americans needlessly killed from March 2020, when the pandemic started in the US, to the November 2020 election.

This caused extreme polarization in America, causing over 50% of Americans to ignore prudent social distancing and mask-wearing guidance, which could have saved 90%–95% of the more than one million Americans who were unjustly and unnecessarily killed by Covid-19.

A moral and caring US president during the Covid-19 pandemic could have saved 980,000 American lives between 2020 and 2022. Let me put it another way: nearly one million Americans are not with us today because of Donald Trump's intentionally divisive tactics.

Before a vaccine was produced, democratic countries like South Korea, Canada, Australia, Taiwan, and others had very low levels of deaths from Covid-19 because their leaders were truthful, caring, and concerned for the best interests of all their people. So there were many countries where humankind came together to *win* the Great Win-win out of love and respect for one another, but the USA was not one of those countries.

This is where the Economic Gospel for the USA comes in, as a way to put America back on the side of the many, not the few, to pave the way for the greatest win-win of all.

The Economic Gospel for the USA makes all the people in your family, in your neighborhood, city, state, the US, and the world winners together because inclusion and diversity are structural benefits and resources for innovating and creating sustainable solutions for current and future generations.

Just like including a diverse portfolio of stocks protects investors from experiencing significant losses over the course of their investment history, so too is it important to include the "We" and the "All" in economic and policy decisions that impact our neighborhoods, cities, states, and country, over the long term, protecting our communities, cities, states, and country from losses and catastrophes that we can't predict.

The Economic Gospel for the USA does not see exploiters as the enemy, whether they are rich and powerful (Grifters), poor and powerless (Freeloaders), or the brainwashed victims of exploiters. The best outcome for America is for exploiters to be understood, held accountable and included as valuable contributors to society.

No person, group, company, or country is trash, garbage, "them," "other," or less than! We all have a role and serve a vital purpose. The question is, do we have the patience, creativity, persistence and will to discover how we are much better together rather than fussing and fighting with each other in our separate ideological corners?

How do we muster the creativity, patience, and empathy to deal with others' everyday issues, roadblocks, and terrors as if we were experiencing them physically and emotionally in our everyday lives?

How can we change our perspectives? How do we muster up the faith and courage to believe that the extra effort required to understand others who do not look, think and behave like us is worth the time of getting to know and learn from them because the opportunities and discoveries created from that investigative effort have the potential to create solutions for all of mankind that will exceed our wildest expectations?

In life, problems and roadblocks spark us to use our differences, collectively and synergistically, like an orchestra, to create solutions beyond our wildest dreams.

We miss the opportunity to create the miraculous when we throw others away because we see them as burdens or things to be exploited for our benefit at their expense or even destruction.

The Economic Gospel for the USA believes exploiters and victims are desirable and need to be won over to create the most successful and sustainable win-win for all. No one's views, ideas, and opinions are too wild to be included. However, those ideas, proposals, and solutions will have to compete and hold up with reality and solutions that create the best and most sustainable value for the greatest amount of people in the group, city, state or country.

••

Great things are possible. For example, only in America could the people freely and willfully elect a person to be the leader of the most wealthy and powerful country on the planet, whose ancestors were the victims of the most brutal form of slavery, segregation, and discrimination that the world has ever known, for 350 years of the 405 years that America has existed.

In any other country on this planet, the minority and tragically victimized populations would have used its rise to leadership as an opportunity to exact revenge and reparations on the white Americans who so mercilessly and happily benefited from the centuries of exploitation and massive wealth creation at the catastrophic expense of African-Americans in this country.

Another way to phrase the previous statement is that in any other country on this planet, the minority and tragically victimized population would never have had a chance of rising and integrating so seamlessly and fairly within society to have ever mounted the support and respect from the ruling majority to have had any chance of electing their minority candidate as president.

But this is the very nature of America! We the people, in order to form a more "perfect union." Americans are not perfect—far from it!

But at the center of America and in the DNA of every true American citizen is the pledge to serve this idea that we are creating, maintaining, and striving to attain a "more perfect union."

Achieving a more perfect union is like achieving eternal life—there's no end to it! More perfect union is always in a state of flux, a state of change toward the improvement of what has been and what can be if we as a people are willing to:

1. Look at our problems and differences as opportunities to learn from ourselves and from each other.

2. Become better versions of ourselves individually.

3. Become better versions of ourselves collectively.

4. Discover and innovate new ways to use our differences to create synergies and solutions that exceed our wildest expectations.

5. Love ourselves and love each other enough to use our problems and differences as fuel and feedstock for uniting us and improving ourselves individually and collectively.

This is the standard. These are the criteria that we must use to achieve the win-win.

Instead of getting even, dominating, controlling, and exploiting, pursuing a more perfect union shows the truth and reality of human beings striving to be the best versions of themselves, individually and working together to ensure that everyone else has the best opportunities to be the best versions of *them*selves. This creates the enthusiasm, motivation, love, commitment, productivity, and synergies required to create and maintain an entire nation or country that is most powerfully striving to become the best version of itself—a more perfect union for all.

Again, America is nowhere near perfect. But our accomplishments are unmatched in human history because of the foundation and ingredients upon which America developed and has had the courage to act upon so wondrously in the infinitesimally small period of time that America has existed on this planet relative to the other major regions and nations of the world—Europe, China, Russia, India, the Middle East, Africa, South America, etc.

Exploiters and the exploited are suffering from broken hearts. The exploited have lost the ability to be empathetic with themselves or others because of the many disappointments and failures they have experienced in their lives. The exploiters have broken or hardened hearts because they have become spoiled and jaded by the massively excessive wealth and benefits that they have received in life, by so easily reaping those benefits at the direct expense or even destruction of others. Once the non-wealthy or non-powerful exploiters, who purposely make themselves victims, buy into the lies and distortions that some evil or bad group of people caused them to be failures in life, it is almost impossible to get them to admit that their victimhood is based on a lie, because they now use that lie to bolster their self-esteem, make themselves feel superior and use that immoral victimhood to shakedown society for what they want and desire.

This is not to say that there are no real victims in life, who need to be helped, developed and supported. But I am just making the point again that exploiters are not just the rich, wealthy, connected and powerful and of course not all, and I would say many or most rich, wealthy, connected and powerful people and groups are not purposely and immorally exploitive by their very nature.

The Economic Gospel for the USA creates the conditions and the environment for proactively and willfully winning the Great Win-

win by "healing the brokenhearted, restoring sight to the blind, and setting at liberty them that are bruised." The Economic Gospel for the USA challenges the will and the heart of the American people to change and willfully win the best win-win for themselves and for their fiercest competitors, opposition or enemies.

How will the Economic Gospel for the USA achieve all that? The world has been looking for a process that does this for . . . for . . . forever. Yep, keep reading. I will detail the process over the course of the rest of this book. It's a nicely defined and innovative process packaged and provided as a service for all the world to use.

So, keep reading to discover the transformative power of the Economic Gospel for the USA.

CHAPTER ONE

The Economic Gospel for the USA and the

World: Vision/Benefits

In this chapter, we're going to start at the end. I'd like to give you a vision of the aspirational goals and resulting benefits to America and the world that will derive from the Economic Gospel for the USA.

1. The creation and maintenance of a moral and economic US and global economy that works best for everyone. In this context, morality and economics are one. You cannot have one without the other. Remember that old saying: "Don't get mad if exploited in a business transaction. It's not personal. It's just business." The new saying will be, "The Great Win-win means business *is* personal."

   We must include the personal as a resource and motivating factor for sparking innovation and harnessing the full diversity of our population. Business being personal is the bright shining light and criteria added to the pot to truly win the Great Win-win for all. Moral economics is not just the goal but the absolute requirement—moral or good ends achieved through moral and good means.

   What will this win-win recipe do? Check out this menu:

a. It creates a quantum leap in the US economic comparative advantage—the lowest business input costs on the planet, motivating and supporting all the nations of the world to follow. Moral economic capitalism—"The Economic Gospel for the USA, Baby!"

b. Builds out the world's best and lowest-cost supply chains (given the structurally lowest-cost environment created above), causing the US labor force participation rate to surge to and remain at all-time record high levels of 75%–85%, with the US national unemployment rate falling to a real and sustainable record low level of 1%–2.5%, motivating and supporting all the nations of the world to follow.

c. Eliminates structurally high inflation in the US economy, motivating and supporting all the nations of the world to follow.

d. Creates and maintains economically competitive markets (as opposed to debt-addictive, financially uncompetitive markets that drive structurally high inflation and unaffordable prices) in America.

e. Produces high-quality, reliable, abundant, and <u>affordable</u> market-driven prices for housing, healthcare, education, transportation, insurance, childcare, retirement, and business capital for all Americans that <u>do not require</u> catastrophic and excessive levels of private/public sector borrowing to support consumption/production of these products/services.

f. Creates and maintains competitive economic market-making, harnessing ecosystem-wide blockchain/AI technology at the industry/sector level, and creating structural economic liquidity (balanced supply and demand) vs. financial liquidity as the primary focus and goal for making markets.

g. Eliminates the need for excessive borrowing in the US economy while reducing private/public sector debt levels from the current catastrophic 380% of US GDP levels to healthy and much more sustainable 130%–150%. The US current account deficit will trade between zero and up to a positive 1% of US GDP, motivating and supporting all the nations of the world to follow.

2. The elimination of democracy-destroying polarization in America and around the world through the use of ICU technology: You, me, and we—social media used the right way!

3. Reimagining and transforming the US K-12 public education system by harnessing "win-win entrepreneurialism" in a project-based learning framework from which annual curriculum and daily lesson plans are directly and dynamically created every day—equipping and inspiring students to develop and love their unique identity/culture, discover and master their superpowers and passionately pursue how and where they can best use their superpowers and unique personalities to make the world a better place, precisely because of their unique contributions.

a. Education, entertainment, and information technology industries work together synergistically to make the K-12 public learning process orders of magnitude more engaging, competitive, inspiring, entertaining, and exciting than what students experience when they attend Disney, Six Flags, and major sports or concert events.

b. The creation of these conditions and resources in US K-12 public schools will have students waking up and going to sleep, thinking and strategizing about how fast they can get back to school the next morning or how they can stay at school longer.

4. A moral and economic US economy going forward that eliminates the catastrophic destruction associated with climate change. Let me explain. Uneconomic financialization of the US and global economy over the past fifty years has caused planet-destroying greenhouse gas emissions in the US economy. This is also the underlying source of the tragic level of polarization in America and around the world. Keeping economics and morality joined at the hip will directly incentivize a robust, sustainable, thriving and zero greenhouse gas emissions environment in the US and around the world.

Now I ask you, do you feel it? Do you taste it? Let these four aspirational goals and resulting benefits sink into your mind, into your spirit, and into your soul. You're probably thinking, Wait a minute. What's going on here? I feel something here. Something like . . . truth . . . or something that really has the potential to be truth . . . something really worthy of our adoration and faith . . . connecting the universe, God, good, and morality to economics, science, and our everyday lives and behaviors . . .

I call this the Economic Gospel for the USA! HALLELUJAH! CAN I GET A WITNESS!

As I discussed in the introduction, America's Constitution provides the guidelines, figuratively speaking, for creating heaven on earth. The issue and problem with America is that Americans have acted and continue to act in ways that do not align with the Constitution. Americans or groups of Americans' desire to exploit and accumulate catastrophically excessive levels of wealth and power at the expense or even destruction of other Americans is a fundamental stain on America. Let's not forget that exploitation is not only driven by the rich, powerful and well connected. The poor, powerless and unconnected can use their powerlessness as a weapon, falsely calling themselves victims of the wealthy and powerful or victims of anything or anyone that they can falsely make a case for and reap significant benefits for their own selfish needs, lusts/desires at the expense or even destruction of others.

What is the nature of the exploitation motive that eats away at American society and the world like a malignant cancer that is hidden, or we're blinded from seeing, even though our eyes are wide open?

Let's go find the moral factor that sits at the core of human behavior. We want to identify, capture, and embed in the very essence of the Economic Gospel for the USA, a foundational principle that keeps us moral. A criterion so clear and so simple, it serves as a shining light to guide our decision-making as it relates to economics, science, relationships, and so on. To accomplish this, I am going to create an allegory: "a story, poem, or picture that can be interpreted to reveal a hidden meaning, typically a moral or political one . . . a complete narrative that seems to be about one thing but is actually about another."

Since we are looking for a story or narrative that many people associate with the beginning, the source of truth and morality, we will use portions of the creation story as the basis for grounding the Economic Gospel for the USA in and making it inseparable from morality.

I recommend we start, metaphorically, at the beginning, the story of creation: free will and morality. I have created an allegory based on the creation story that I call "the Misinterpretation of Eve," which, metaphorically, establishes a firm foundation for understanding the proper role of free will and freedom in defining what America is and how all Americans can willfully fall in love with being American in America once again—the foundation of the Economic Gospel for the USA.

CHAPTER TWO

The Misinterpretation of Eve
(The Woke Half of Man: Wo-Man)

In the Biblical creation story, God's ultimate goal was to make humankind in the image and likeness of God. God promised Adam and Eve that they could live forever in a perfect world without envy, strife, poverty, or unmet needs if they refrained from eating from the Tree of the Knowledge of Good and Evil. In the his-story interpretation of the creation story, Eve is the "villain" and "weaker vessel" of humankind. Eve gave in to her lustful and envious desires to want to be like or equal with God and decided to eat from the Tree of the Knowledge of good and evil—bringing sin, death, and destruction into a world that had been peaceful. God then cursed Eve for her envious disobedience by making all females experience the excruciating pain and suffering that comes with childbirth and raising a family. I believe this is the his-story interpretation of the creation story, which I call the misinterpretation of Eve.

In what I call the "correct" interpretation of the creation story, the her-story interpretation of the creation story, Eve is actually the hero, becoming the vessel through which God achieves his/her ultimate goal for humankind. God rewards and blesses Eve for her revolutionary and courageous act by anointing Eve and all females with the gift of demonstrating and leading willful moral unity for humankind.

Willful moral unity is the highest expression of God's love, often described as Godly or Agape love. Willful moral unity is the act of having the full knowledge of what is right and what is wrong and choosing to do right every time, even when you have the option, every time, to choose wrong, where doing wrong is almost always the easier thing to do, with many, many more benefits accruing to you personally, but usually at the expense, harm, or even destruction of many others.

Eve's decision to eat from the Tree of the Knowledge of Good and Evil was not a sign of some naturally depraved weakness in the female species' DNA or some selfish and envious lustful desire to be better than or compete with God for power and control over the universe. Eve was making herself a vessel through which God would complete his/her promise to humankind—that promise being that man (male and female) were created in the image and the likeness of God.

Prior to Eve eating from the Tree of the Knowledge of Good and Evil, Adam and Eve were both much more like robots than human beings. Without knowing what is right and wrong, Adam and Eve had no ability to exercise the powers of free will that God had given them. They had no basis for evaluating whether their actions were right or wrong.

This ability to distinguish between good and evil, and then additionally and most importantly, having the power to choose good every time, even though the option to choose evil is always present, is the most distinctive characteristic of what it means to be

God or be like God, which was God's ultimate desire and promise to humankind.

God created Eve, a female, to be a helpmate or partner to man, helping him to see and do things he could not see and do on his own. Eve could clearly see that humankind, both male and female, were far from being anything close to "being like God," and she knew and could see clearly that God's heart and desire was that the creation of humankind (male and female) be in the image and likeness of God. Eve read between the lines of the promise of God. If humankind cannot distinguish between good and evil, there is no way that the character and essence of humankind could even remotely resemble the image and likeness of God.

God promised Adam and Eve that if they ate the fruit of the Tree of the Knowledge of Good and Evil, they would be like God, knowing good and evil. But God also promised that if they ate from the Tree of the Knowledge of Good and Evil, they would lose eternal life and the security of the peaceful world of the Garden of Eden, where all their wants and needs were satisfied and where they never had to worry about envy, strife, fighting, stealing or killing - forever!

Eve's decision to eat from the fruit of the Tree of Knowledge was a "willful" act of pure love. By eating from the Tree of the Knowledge of Good and Evil, Eve opens the door through which God completes his promise to humankind. Eve's decision was an act of "willful" pure love because Eve could have remained safe and ***conservative***, protecting her gift of eternal life and of living in the Garden of Eden, where all of her wants and needs for life remained protected for forever. This "willful" choice, Eve's Choice, was God-like and affirmed God's decision to give Adam a helpmate or partner to help humankind become more like God.

Now, it's one thing to have the knowledge of Good and Evil; it's an entirely different matter, effort, or issue to have the moral integrity to decide to do good every time, like God does when making a choice between doing right or wrong. God gave Eve the "gift" of demonstrating to humanity how humankind can choose to do good every time, "like god," as a reward for her courage, love, and faithfulness: giving up eternal life, eternal riches, and security to be the vessel through which God could keep his promise to humankind.

But according to the his-story interpretation of the Bible, God then punished Eve for her disobedience by cursing her with the pain, agony, and suffering associated with childbirth and raising children. How is that a reward?

Well, you must have humility, love, courage, grace, and "wokeness" in your heart and spirit to see this . . . God was not punishing Eve by giving her the responsibility of childbirth and child rearing. God was actually rewarding, blessing, and "promoting" Eve to "lead and manage" the highest and most honorable responsibility in human activity.

The decision to have a child, suffer the pain and misery of the birth process, and then commit to 18–25 years of unwavering and total commitment to the development and raising of a child or children to maturity is as close to the human expression of an act that reflects God's love as any other action or activity in the human experience.

Parents do not profit from raising a family. In economic terms, the true "market cost" of the total services mothers/parents give to each child from birth to maturity is on the order of $1 million per child raised to maturity, with absolutely no expectation of any return on services provided.

What the his-story interpretation of the creation story sees as a curse is actually a blessing in the her-story interpretation. The demonstration of the handiwork of God, or the love of God in its purest form, is clear in the her-story version. The female species of man has in her DNA, because of Eve's love and faithfulness, the ability to create, nurture, develop, and prepare human life for maturity, where that life is then ready to contribute maximally to the life process itself. This creation, bearing, raising, and preparing of children for life is the very expression of God incarnate in the everyday lives and activities of parents raising and providing for their children.

God gave the female the leadership and responsibility for creating and developing life as a reward and blessing for her courage and faithfulness in being the vessel through which God fulfilled his promise to humankind. Eve had the faith, courage, and love to risk and actually give up eternal life and riches and security to serve as God's vessel.

Finally, the childbearing and child-raising process God blessed and rewarded Eve and womankind with produces a kind of leadership that is probably the best model for creating and maintaining unity, camaraderie, and miraculously synergistic teamwork in groups of people, large or small. It takes love, hard work, sacrifice, immense creativity, and investment in time and resources to create and maintain conditions where each member of a group or organization actually has the maximum opportunity to develop and become the best possible version of themselves while simultaneously, synergistically and most effectively meeting organization, group, or community goals (sales levels, profits, net zero carbon emissions, etc.).

But this is exactly what good mothers, or wonderful parents, do for their children. This is why the bond between children and their parents is so strong, passionate, loyal, and proactive. Childbirth and child-raising through maturity do not make economic or business sense. It is pure love; it is part of the life process; it is life itself; it is the handiwork of God. Without it, human life will perish on this planet. Having children and raising them is a choice. Man/womankind can willfully decide not to take up that expensive, non-economic, non-profitable activity. Capitalism would never fund this activity on its own.

The best and happiest groups, organizations, and communities are those whose leadership creates and maintains structures that provide all individual members with the best opportunity to develop and become the best versions of themselves possible. How? By treating, caring for, protecting, and empowering each team member as if they were their own child.

This sounds simplistic, or too prescriptive to put in words or policy. My experience suggests that organizational strife and poor productivity basically and fundamentally derive from an organization's structural lack of opportunities for individual team members to develop and grow into the best possible versions of themselves or leadership/other team members, ignoring or deliberately sabotaging the development and growth opportunities of other team or group members.

True individual human self-actualization is impossible to achieve in isolation. Like Adam and Eve, we all need others to bring out the best in ourselves. By helping others be the best they can be, we are simultaneously helping ourselves to become the best possible versions of ourselves. Think of Michael Jordan, one of the greatest basketball players to ever play the game. MJ would have never reached his level of success and professionalism if there were no Gary Payton,

Magic Johnson, John Stockton, Larry Byrd, etc., other highly skilled professional basketball players pushing him to compete at levels and draw on talents and leadership that he would never have harnessed without the push and challenge of competition from others.

The moral to this story is that in an open and free society, where decision-making is democratic based on people's free will, society can make the best (economic) and moral (right) decisions when all members of society agree to and are actively working together to ensure that everyone in society has the best opportunity to develop and be the best possible versions of themselves. This can be achieved by everyone in society agreeing to treat, care for, protect and develop each other the same way we treat, care for, protect and develop our children.

This is the secret sauce, the criteria and process that the Economic Gospel for the USA uses to ensure that there is no separation between economics and morality. Thank Ya!!

We Are Our Brother's Keeper! We must care for and develop *ourselves* and *others* the same way we care for and develop our *own children*.

"The Misinterpretation of Eve—Creation Story" provides perspective and a great parallel for understanding "The Misinterpretation of American Freedom": what it really means to be an American and what's required to fulfill America's potential and promise to ourselves and to the world community.

CHAPTER THREE

The Misinterpretation of American Freedom

The primary source of America's strength is not her ability to give individual Americans the freedom to do anything they want, however they want to do it, with no concern for how their actions impact others. The goal of America is not freedom. Freedom is not the highest priority and is not the most valued or sacred treasure in America. As a matter of fact, freedom divorced from Americans' love and respect for themselves and love and respect for their fellow Americans is a selfish and divisive cancer on life and American society.

The "true" source of America's strength is the freedom and the will of the American people to prioritize "a more perfect union" as the nation's highest value and highest priority. In the Preamble to the Constitution, you can find the embodiment of the vision, mission, and national strategy statement for America. The Preamble confirms that all Americans have staked their "citizenship" on the belief and commitment that unity for the sake of unity "is not the goal of America," but rather Americans collectively stake their belief and commitment in a "more perfect union for all" Americans *by all* Americans. That is the goal!

The goal of achieving a more "perfect" union implies that Americans work together to create a unity that more effectively captures our diversity, size, and scale synergistically to produce maximum benefits for the nation as a whole and simultaneously produce maximum benefits for individual states, localities, communities, and the individual citizens themselves.

It is human nature for people to want to be part of, support, and work together in unity to make the community better if the result is that both the group and the individuals in the group can thrive and become the best possible versions of themselves. This is precisely because of the proactive and willful teamwork that makes work and outcomes simultaneously best at both the group and individual levels.

Just imagine what America would be like if it had not committed to striving for a more perfect union for all as America's highest priority. Would we have the following collective and vital services and protections that the free market could not and still cannot support on its own?

- Security of the nation, states, cities, and communities from threats domestic and international
- Protection, support, and recovery from weather and environmental catastrophes
- Product and service health and safety standards, protections and enforcements
- Public education and public health services
- Retirement safety net support services
- Computers, the internet
- Hydraulic fracking
- Electricity, lights, fuel industry (coal, oil, natural gas, solar, wind)

- Cell phones, airplanes, automobiles, food and agriculture

The above list of protections and services is not perfect because we are not perfect. That is precisely why our goal, our highest priority, and our highest value should be the relentless pursuit of a "more perfect union," the process that gets closer and better over time at producing services and fulfilling needs that are met for everyone at the best possible level of quality and affordability.

None of these great services and industries could have started or survived without the collective effort of the private and public sectors (government) working hand in hand together, sharing knowledge, resources, and collective aspirations and visions of the future to make those services and industries a reality over many years of smart, hard, dedicated and gracious effort. Dr. Martin Luther King Jr. was assassinated in 1968, but exactly forty years later, Barack Obama was elected President of the United States of America. We ain't perfect, but the speed, quality, and number of people included in our progress totally depend on us.

This shows precisely why "Freedom in and of itself is not the highest value or most important goal for Americans in America." Freedom isolated from its contexts and impact on other human beings is divisive and destructive, ultimately leading to a win-lose, or worse, a lose-lose minimalist approach and outcome for life. But freedom wrapped in a more perfect union for all maximizes the opportunity for everyone, creating an economy and society that works best for everyone in both the short and long term. This type of freedom can only be created by and from a unity that is based on a more perfect union for all, one that creates collective synergy and productivity so that everyone can experience true freedom both at the individual and collective levels.

That is why we are called the United States of America! Not the Individual States of America, not the Free and Independent States of America, not the Liberal States of America, not the Conservative States of America, not the God-Fearing States of America, not the Capitalistic States of America—we are the ***United*** States of America.

Remember Michael Jordan? As we discussed previously, MJ would not have risen to the heights of excellence that he achieved playing professional basketball had there not been other super-great basketball players who challenged and pushed him to develop and achieve his level of greatness. We can only be truly free and reach the best version of ourselves possible if we simultaneously create and maintain an economy and society where everyone else can be the best version of themselves. We become our best when we ensure everyone else is becoming and achieving their best too. *E Pluribus Unum*, baby!

The beauty of striving for a more perfect union is that there is an explicit understanding that "change" is the only constant that does not change. Constant change is baked into the cake.

Maintaining a more perfect union is a target that is always in flux. Our ability to work together in ways that allow both individual citizens and the nation as a whole to continually have the ability to be the best versions of ourselves possible absolutely requires an evolving flexibility in our very character and relationship with one another.

The premises and assumptions for how and why we work together to maintain a more perfect union today may or may not be the same as those premises and assumptions that were used in the past or may be used in the future. What does not change is the goal of maintaining a more perfect union so that all Americans as a nation and all Americans as individual citizens have and maintain the best possible opportunities for being the best possible versions of themselves, *for* all Americans *by* all Americans.

What has to happen (morally and economically) to make this happen, and how it has to happen (morally and economically), is the beauty, creativity, passion, love, and commitment that make America American. In short, **IT'S ALL ABOUT MEE!**

••

True democracy is synonymous with **MEE: Morality, Economics and Entrepreneurialism**.

Morality implies we, everybody, all Americans, past, present, and future, should be included in the equation when considering how Americans work together to achieve a more perfect union that works best for everyone. Not just for the successful and winners in life, not just out of sympathy, concern, and help for the less fortunate or the true victims in life. Morality includes, plans, and prepares for all Americans—Black, white, yellow, red, rich, poor, Jew, Gentile, just and unjust.

Economics is synonymous with democracy in the sense that the best solutions for the nation as a whole and the best solutions for all the individuals who make up the nation are best achieved through integrating short- and long-term economics. This establishes the most productive, synergistic, and affordable paths for operating the US economy and American society in ways that work best for everyone.

Today and over the course of American history, wealth creation for the winners in society has primarily driven how the economy grows and how American society behaves. This explains why:

1. Inequality is at its highest level in history today.

2. Polarization in America is at or near its peak level in history today.

3. Climate change is barreling forward at a pace that is on course to destroy our planet for future generations of humans on this planet in the next 5 to 10 years if the status quo of the last fifty years persists going forward.

History has demonstrated emphatically that we have not learned from our past economic mistakes because we keep repeating them and allowing the rot to fester, not because of a lack of knowledge or experience, but rather because of a lack of love, will, and care for each other as a nation and because of a lack of love, will, and care for each other as individuals. We "Are our Brother's Keeper," and America and Americans' lack of love, concern, and commitment for and to each other explains precisely why the deep holes and gaps in America's economy and America's society persist and are spreading like an uncontrolled cancer, right before our wide open but blinded eyes.

We have become blinded by our freedom to exploit and use our fellow citizens for our catastrophically excessive and greedy benefit at others' expense; it is our intentional and contrived freedom to exploit others and not be held accountable that is destroying American democracy and increasingly sustaining the US economy on a foundation made of sinking sand, likely to collapse at any time. Catastrophe often strikes when we least expect it.

Finally, but equally important, is the spirit of entrepreneurialism. I call this willfully winning the Great Win-win in the US economy and society. Great entrepreneurs are creative problem solvers with an endless supply of empathy; they are always consciously aware of the most important stakeholders associated with the agreement or deal under consideration. They are keenly aware of what stakeholders need and want and understand what would be required to exceed their highest expectations.

Great entrepreneurs also have an exceptional grasp on reality and what is available and can realistically consummate the deal. This clear grasp of reality is not a limitation that makes it more difficult to meet the competing objectives of the various stakeholders. Having a firm grasp on reality and knowing what you have to work with gives great entrepreneurs the power of focus and the ability to graciously create and reinvent options for satisfying stakeholders' wants/needs beyond their wildest imagination.

If solutions 1, 2, 3, 4, and 5 do not work, that does not mean a solution is not achievable. What it really means is that those unsatisfactory solutions 1, 2, 3, 4, and 5 are actually gifts from God, road maps of instruction that show entrepreneurs how to change their approach so that solution #6 is the agreement or deal winner, not only meeting stakeholder requirements but also exceeding stakeholders' wildest expectations, wherever possible.

This spirit of entrepreneurialism is not just for businesspeople but for all Americans in terms of how we interact with and treat one another as we decide how we are going to live, work, and play together in the economy and in society, as we create and maintain our more perfect union.

Again, freedom in the context of America is more of a result or an outcome of the collective "we for me." My individual freedom and power are actually optimized by my willful and willing commitment and desire to work with other Americans to discover how our collective efforts to make our union or agreements more perfect actually maximize my individual opportunities and powers to be the best version of myself possible. This is the proper interpretation of American freedom.

So if America's highest value and highest priority is a "more perfect union," why is America being ravaged with disunity and polarization at levels not seen since the Civil War? Because many Americans are falling and have fallen out of love with being American to themselves and to others. America and Americans fail to be American when they/we prioritize the love of or the lust for wealth, power, influence, and control over our love and commitment for creating and maintaining a more perfect union for all Americans. There is really a lot of truth in that old saying: "The love of money is the root of all evil." Lies, distortions and victimizations separate Americans and pit them against one another, and that saps America's strength, power, and legitimacy at its core.

Exploitative behavior creates great wealth, power, influence, and fame for the exploiters in society who perpetrate lies and distortions to gain and maintain a significant and unfair advantage in life. However, the very real moral, economic, and social cancers created by these lies and distortions will eventually wipe out the catastrophically excessive gains and benefits that were achieved at the expense of America and its democracy. Therefore, it is imperative that America and all Americans take the initiative both now and going forward to save American democracy by proactively being American to each other and the rest of the world, winning the Great Win-win by working together with all other Americans to create and maintain a more perfect union for all Americans—by caring for, protecting, supporting, and treating each other the same way we care for, protect, support, and treat our own children.

This is the proper interpretation of American freedom. We the people of the United States, in order to form a more perfect union, E Pluribus Unum! WE = ME!

OK, great, so now what? The Economic Gospel for the USA is Here . . . But . . .

CHAPTER FOUR

When America Fails to Be American:

Problem Identification

- Moral Hazards and Economic Cancer
- Americans in Love with Eating Africans
- Americans in Love with Eating Itself
- Ukraine
- Global Pandemics
- Former President Donald Trump
- The Source of Inflation in the US Economy
- The Ultimate Con Game

Moral Hazards and Economic Cancer

Moral hazards are "a situation where an economic actor has an incentive to increase its exposure to risk because it does not bear the full costs of that risk." In relation to the Economic Gospel for the USA, I define a moral hazard as:

"An economic actor's decision to relentlessly increase and repeat catastrophically exploitative behaviors on others because they know they will not be held accountable for their catastrophic exploitation."

The problem with this statement and the concept of moral hazard is that it does not tell the entire story. Let's expand the concept by looking at a universal law in physics that applies directly and specifically to every aspect of life and reality in the universe—Newton's Third Law of Physics: "For every action, there is an equal and opposite reaction." So, how does this law or principle of the universe apply to the socioeconomic principle of moral hazard?

My View

People or groups who exploit others outside their group to gain excessive wealth, power and control or to protect and keep excessive levels of wealth, power, and control at the expense of or even destruction of others outside their group eventually become so lustfully addicted to this exploitative behavior that when they have sucked all the exploitative juices out of the other group, they will turn this exploitative behavior on their own group, themselves—in effect, they become willing to "eat on" (exploit) members of their own group to satisfy their lust for increased wealth, power and control or to prevent losing massive levels of wealth, power and control previously obtained through past exploitations.

This definition of moral hazard demonstrates the consequences of unaccounted-for moral hazards. The dangers of moral hazards are that the person or group exploiting others and getting away with it (which is what moral hazard means by definition) thinks that Newton's Third Law of Physics does not apply to them. Wrong! Newton's Third Law of Physics applies to all matter in the universe, living or inanimate. This is what makes moral hazards so dangerous. There is the illusion that if you are an exploiter, you have power and control to exploit others, and there is no visible power or entity to hold you accountable for your exploitation. You may begin to believe that Newton's Third Law of Physics is not real or does not apply to social and economic behavior. Wrong!

The consequences of moral hazards or unaccounted for exploitative behavior:

1. An unquenchable desire to repeat and increase exploitation levels in the future, precisely because the behavior was and is not being held to account currently or in the past.

2. Hardens the exploiter's heart, creating lies, distortions, and conspiracy theories to justify exploitative behavior.

3. Exploiters' hardened hearts prevent them from seeing or feeling the catastrophic effects of their exploitative behavior on the exploited group/population and also blind them from seeing and feeling when the result of their exploitative behavior begins to negatively or even catastrophically affect members of the exploiting group or population (when exploiters begin exploiting or eating themselves).

As I will show later in the text, unaccounted for moral hazards are actually accounted for by Newton's Third Law of Physics and are described above in Steps 2 and 3. The very nature of the exploitative process creates a physical and economic imbalance that may not appear in the raw economic and social fundamentals explicitly tracked in the literature. However, the cumulative impact of these imbalances will eventually spill over and flood our economy and society with an equal and opposite reaction built up from Newton's

Third Law over time. In Biblical terms, this is the age-old verse: we will eventually reap what we have sown!

Moral hazard behavior is so seductively addictive that when the exploiting group can no longer exploit the "other" or the "them" group, it will turn on itself and create many crazy distortions, rationales, and conspiracy theories to make their tragic exploitative behavior "justified and true" in order to con their own people or group into believing that the exploitation being done to them is good, just and in their moral and economic interest/benefit.

Moral hazard unaccountability is a legacy that America has written and has been acting out over the course of its history to this very day. But . . .

THIS DOES NOT HAVE TO BE AMERICA'S LEGACY!

America and Americans, if we proactively, willfully, and willingly fall in love with being American to ourselves, to each other, and to our fellow citizens of the world, by being accountable and responsible for our cumulative moral hazards, we will and we can have and will achieve what the "Great Prayer" aspires for all humankind on this planet—". . . On earth as it is in Heaven."

As I will show later in the book, America and Americans can and will become accountable and responsible for our cumulative moral hazards by putting into practice the Economic Gospel for the USA.

This is not a negative view of America, although when reading this, some may think that is the purpose of this section. No, no and Hell to the no! The purpose of this section is to identify the structural problems in US society and the American economy so that we can more clearly and accurately describe what the solution should be and how we achieve that solution. If we sugarcoat identifying what the core problems are in American society and the US economy, our solution and strategy for success will be irrelevant and useless. So like Samuel Jackson said in the first Jurassic Park movie, "Hold your butts," because here we go!

••

Americans in Love with Eating Africans

For America, the 800-million-pound elephant in the room is the slavery, segregation and discrimination of Africans in this country—with the full weight and support of the federal, state and local governments enforcing the laws that protected the maintenance and stability of these institutions for 350 years.

This was done specifically for the massively excessive wealth benefit of white Americans at the direct and catastrophic expense, economic, social and physical destruction, of African immigrants only. Slavery for 250 years and then segregation and discrimination legally for another 100 years—these horribly immoral institutions (slavery, segregation, and discrimination) created, maintained and protected by the wonderful and beautiful principles that we have discussed, embodied in the US Preamble and the Constitution of the United States? How in the world were those dreadfully un-American institutions allowed to persist for so long in America? Not because the principles in the US government and constitution are flawed, but because the people in charge of the government were not holding themselves accountable to the principles and intentions embodied in American law.

In my opinion, this is not an issue of race. But when you look at how slavery, segregation and discrimination were implemented in America, you would have to say, Stop fooling yourself. It was all about race, right? How was it that in just 270 years, America could grow to become the wealthiest and most powerful country on this planet, when all the other large and powerful countries of the world have been on this planet for many tens of thousands of years? Answer: The most brutal form of slavery and exploitation free labor of African immigrants only, in the history of the world.

The sale of cotton, sugar cane, tobacco, etc. that was grown and packaged with free slave labor in the South and sent to the North, where these raw materials were used in factories to create products that were used in America and shipped all over the world, creating profit margins for white Americans only, which both touched the skies and kissed heaven's doors.

The massively crazy profits from agriculture, made possible by the immoral and brutal slave labor of African immigrants only, funded America's Industrial Revolution of the mid- to late 1800s. In today's dollars, slave labor, not including compensation for pain and suffering, which could and should rightfully double or triple these numbers, would be on the order of $20–$30 trillion dollars. To be conservative, let's say that it's $25 trillion. If these funds were equally distributed to every African-American today, that distribution would be $610,000 per African-American citizen or about $2.4 million for every African-American family.

A few paragraphs ago, I started this discussion by saying the issues that we are speaking about here are not about race. Yet, it seems that every other sentence that I have written since seems to be about nothing but race.

Not true. I am actually demonstrating a point.

IT'S NOT ABOUT RACE!

It's not about race. It is about the immoral and exploitive economic and social violation forced on one specific group of people, African immigrants only, who white Americans exploited purely for their massive economic benefit, not because of the color of the skin of Africans but because they had the power, the freedom and the absolute ability to do so for 350 years for their own selfish and massive economic and social benefit.

This was an act powered by the will of human nature. If the roles were reversed, and Africans were importing white people into Africa with the power and the freedom to enslave them and have the opportunity to create such massively incredible wealth in only 270 years in order to become the wealthiest and most powerful country on the planet, the African people in African countries would have willingly and purposely decided to savagely exploit white immigrants only, in the same manner that white people in America savagely exploited African immigrants only.

The issue is not about skin color, race or culture. The actual issue here is about the extreme and immoral economic and social violation of a group of people who happened to all be African immigrants only, not because they were African, not because they had brown skin, and not because they had different facial and hair features. The reason Africans were so maliciously exploited was because they were powerless, under the thumb and foot of the American government and the American people who happened to be white in this situation.

Now the extreme economic and social violation needs to be corrected, not because of race but because only African immigrants were economically and morally raped and castrated, very significantly and directly disadvantaging African-Americans only, as a people, to this day in terms of accumulated economic, financial and social wealth, employment and entrepreneurial opportunities in America and around the world, relative to white Americans.

There is a direct reason and cause for why in 2024 the group of people in America who are the lowest on the wealth scale, lowest on the education scale and the highest on the poverty, crime and poor health scale are African-Americans. Uncompensated for and the unaccounted for moral hazards associated with slavery, segregation and discrimination in America for 350 years perfectly explain why African-Americans, as a people, struggle so profusely in America, relative to white Americans. Again, this has nothing to do with race but everything to do with what was purposely inflicted on African immigrants only, which puts them 350 years behind in the economic and financial race and competition for vibrant and successful life in the world's most wealthy and successful economy.

If you have great wealth, on average, the chances are hugely in your favor of getting a good K-12 education, college education, great development exposure, and role models growing up. If you have wealth, you have a much better chance of meeting people, traveling, experiencing the culture and different people in your community and around the country or even around the world, experiencing your ultimate profession while in high school and college, meeting people who are successful, role models, understanding finance and how to plan and invest, etc. This is especially true if you have had this wealth and exposure in your family over multiple generations.

Are there people who start from nothing and become wealthy and successful? Of course. But reality and the numbers don't lie.

As a people, the ratio between black and white wealth is still catastrophic. The ratio before the civil rights movement, in 1950, was 7 to 1. Today, in 2024, that ratio has only narrowed to 6.45 to 1. Today, if the median net wealth of an African-American family is about $60,000, the median net wealth for a white family is $387,000.

Today, African-Americans are twice as likely to have committed crimes and be in jail as whites and have performed or achieved only half as well as whites in academic pursuits.

So after being together for 405 years in this country, why do these massive gaps in wealth, education and achievement persist between African-American and white families in America? Are African-Americans innately inferior? Are white Americans innately superior?

The best science, sociologists and our current laws today suggest that society should not discriminate based on race or the color of one's skin because, in the eyes of the law, in terms of our innate capabilities, we are all equal as people. And I agree with that. But if that is true, then why do we still have basically the same level of wealth and health outcome gaps between African-American and white Americans today as in 1950, before the start of the world-famous Civil Rights movement in America?

Because it's not about race or the natural inferiority of the African-American people.

Then what is it? You know what it is; we know what it is. It's obvious in the context of this discussion. It's the deliberate, aggressive, intentional and extreme social and economic immoral violation of African immigrants only by the full weight, intention and agreement of the American government and the white American people for 350 years, directly and deliberately for their own selfish benefit and enrichment. The wealth gap between whites and African-American people in America goes away if African-Americans are justly compensated for slavery, segregation and discrimination. Remember, if reparations were paid based on the economic value of services provided by African immigrants only, free slave labor to this country, each African American family in America would receive a check for $2.4 million dollars. If those checks were cut and sent to African American families today, the economic and social inequality gaps between African-Americans and White Americans would decrease drastically over the course of a year and disappear over the course of the next five years. Those checks would not be a handout. They would not be welfare. They would not be socialism. Those checks would be justified compensation for African Americans who made it absolutely possible for America rise from nothing to the most powerful and wealthy country on this planet in only 270 years. A miracle, right? No, a 350-year exploitive rape and robbery of excessively exploited human effort, pocketed and enjoyed by and for white Americans only in America.

Again, I repeat, the issue is not race. It's about the exploitation that was done to a specific group of people, because the exploiters had the power and will to exploit that group without having to pay for it economically and without fear of the law or legal system holding them accountable. I believe that this is human nature, and if Africans were in a similar position and able to exploit white immigrants only in Africa, under similar circumstances, they would have done the same things to white Europeans, not because they are white, but because of the crazy amount of wealth and power that could have been created, maintained and controlled through such exploitation in such a short period of time.

However, this does not justify the exploitation!

Just because all humans have the capacity to exploit does not make it right and does not mean that the violation does not have to be rectified. It should be rectified because of the violations and the damage that it has inflicted on the people who were violated and the damage that it has done to the exploiting population, morally, economically and competitively as a people. The unforeseen catastrophic effects of unaccounted for moral hazards will be described and demonstrated in the next section of this book. It sneaks up on us because we are so blinded from seeing it because of our absolute commitment to and allegiance to maintaining existing and creating new, unaccounted for moral hazards.

Today's resistance to governmental social and economic support based on the color of African-Americans's skin is 100% correct. But what is also true is that African-Americans in America should be supported and given preference economically and socially because of the catastrophic economic and social violations against them for 350 years, which shows up very clearly and distinctly in the raw economic, wealth, health, social, educational and crime comparisons between whites and African-Americans in America today. The only reason those gaps persist today is because of the unaccounted-for economic and moral hazards that have been ignored and not corrected sufficiently to this day.

African-Americans deserve this government support not because of the color of their skin but because of the supernaturally massive economic contributions that they made to America through their 250 years of free slave labor and another hundred years of segregation and discrimination, preventing Africans from competing on a level playing field with other American citizens, not just 200 years ago, not just 100 years ago, and not just 50 years ago, but today and well into the future, depending on what is done to correct this economic moral hazard that is very much alive and kicking today.

This is not vengeance, hate, laziness, or looking for a handout. This is purely economic and social compensation for a job well done by African-Americans, creating extraordinary value added to America through slavery, segregation and discrimination.

Again, I am not talking about the solutions yet. We are still identifying the problem. I am not saying that a check giving every African American family in America $2.4 million is the solution.

Remember, if we do not look the problem in the face and deal with it, an effective solution will never come forth. Our more perfect union will seem ineffective and not worth striving for because we do not want to face the truth and the impacts of our past in the context of their reality and their real-life impact on all the people of the United States of America, not just the privileged few.

So now let's look at the second part of the negative effects of allowing moral hazards to persist and go unaccounted for.

What we have discussed in the context of American economic history is a major example of the negative effects on a group of people being exploited by an unaccounted for moral hazard: Africans, enslaved for 250 years, then segregated and discriminated against for another hundred years following slavery, legally and fully supported by the weight, power and enforcement of the most powerful and wealthy country on this planet with the overwhelming support of the majority of the white people who made up America, for their own selfish economic and financial benefit at the expense and destruction of African immigrants only.

Greed is a human motive found in all humans, not in any way only associated just with white Americans. However, since white Americans chose to act on that instinct, history and the laws of science, social science, economics demand that accountability for those actions and justice be granted to those who were violated. Or what? That is what we will discuss now.

Again, this is not a negative story about America or a negative story about white people in America. This is a story about redemption. And the fundamental first step to redemption is recognizing and acknowledging the immoral behaviors we knowingly committed. Confirmation of this acknowledgement can be demonstrated by compensating those we have wronged and showing a commitment to never repeating these wrongs in the future.

We can't ignore this because of what we are about to discuss now, which explains precisely why the wealth gap between blacks and whites persists so stubbornly after 405 years together.

Unaccounted-for economic moral hazards engender an insatiable addiction to continuing to repeat the immoral behavior. This perpetuates a cycle of exploitation, with the exploiter reaping massive benefits from exploitative behaviors at the expense and even the destruction of those being exploited.

Unaccounted-for economic moral hazards are like "crack to a crack addict"—once you get started, it is very hard and seemingly almost impossible to stop. And what is the fate or destiny of crack addicts who continue to increase their insatiable habit? You already know . . .

So the second negative effect of unaccounted-for moral hazards is not only the damage done to those who are exploited but also the insatiable addiction to continue or repeat the moral hazardous behavior, which, if continued, *will not only continue to negatively affect and destroy the exploited group or population but also negatively impact and destroy the exploiters themselves.*

Let's look at another couple of examples of this in US economic history.

Again, remember, this is the problem identification portion of the text, not America-bashing. When I was growing up, this was called "tough love," without which you get children who are spoiled, entitled, afraid to experiment, afraid to step out on faith and learn from their failures. In my experience with families that have children and young adults who have not been given the benefits of tough love when the storms of life come their way and they are no longer under the love and protection of their parents, these kids are most susceptible to depression, drug abuse, poor social skills and poor relationships, mental illness and suicides.

We don't want this outcome individually or sociologically in American society, so let's press on!

When we get to the solution part of the book, we will have some great context and perspective on what the solution should look like and why, because we didn't sugarcoat things in our problem identification analysis for fear of what we would find.

Americans in Love with Eating Itself: Unaccounted-for cumulative moral hazards

In addition to the $25 trillion in free labor that Africans provided America to directly fuel and empower its miraculous rise to become the most powerful nation on the planet, in just 270 years, America has also been blessed with almost unlimited energy resources to grow its economy at a significant advantage relative to the rest of the world. That is, until the early 1950s.

Early in the 1950s, scientists and economists in the energy industry discovered that, for the first time in American history, America's economy was on the precipice of being challenged by a nationwide energy shortage. At this point in time, the massively large and fast-growing US economy was almost 99% powered by oil and natural gas energy supplies.

American energy scientists and economists discovered that the oil and natural gas supplies in the US economy would peak in twenty years, i.e., by 1970, if America did not 1) find new ways to produce more oil and gas, 2) create different types of energy to power the economy as a substitute for oil and natural gas shortages, and 3) slow the economy down so that our economic growth did not exceed the energy needed to power it.

Business and political interests in the energy industry were not pleased with these predictions or the actions that might be required to prevent the catastrophic conditions that would occur if the largest, wealthiest and most powerful country on the planet were for the first time in its history, constrained by a lack of energy resources. These abundant, seemingly endless energy resources had always been assumed to be ready and available for use to America, as the one place on this planet with a seemingly unlimited supply of energy for its economy.

Because energy supplies and energy prices are the starting point of everything that works and functions in the economy, a sustained structural shortage in oil and natural gas supplies in the US economy would have been catastrophic for America, fundamentally destroying America's comparative advantage in the world and creating real pain and absolute destruction to the lives of the majority of Americans, whose abilities and opportunities to enjoy the fruits of American life would be significantly negatively impacted for current and future generations of Americans.

In the early 1950s, America was benefiting from tens of billions of dollars in international trade associated with the rebuilding efforts after the destruction in Europe related to World War II. America was still riding high from its leadership and support efforts in the war and the pride and patriotism that resulted from that leadership and support, both in America and around the world. Federal funds were being liberally supplied to war veterans through the GI Bill to finance education, purchase homes and start new businesses. The cost of living was so low in America at that time that the typical family could live on the income of one parent while the other parent remained at home, raising the family and providing a stable, safe and congenial community and culture for American families. On all metrics, America was leading or near the top in terms of quality of life indicators. Education, per capita income and wealth, recreation and entertainment resources, robust industry and manufacturing growth, good-paying union jobs, with fully paid pension benefits— this is the period of time that former president Donald Trump is always referring to when he says, "Let's make America great again."

Now the stage is set, in the early 1950s, arguably when America was as great as it has ever been, for our "good red-blooded," loyal, patriotic and faithful American citizens, surely . . . surely . . . surely—the American energy industry, its associated manufacturing and business interests, patriotic American politicians and the US government—surely they all worked proactively together to warn the American public about the catastrophic threat and risk to the US economy and America's wonderful way of life if the economists' and scientists' predictions about peak oil and natural gas production were to come true in the next fifteen to twenty years?

Logically, morally and economically, from the standpoint of what would be best for all Americans, and especially for the "good red-blooded," loyal, patriotic and faithful American citizens, a nation-wide campaign to diversify America's energy resources and/or to discover new ways to increase oil and natural gas production in America by 1970 should have been priority #1, given the catastrophic and permanent consequences of not preparing for this risk. Right?

Would there be any conceivable reason why the American energy industry, its associated businesses, and political and government leaders would not want to lead and inform the American public about the catastrophic risks associated with the predicted peak oil and natural gas production in the US by 1970 and the urgent need for an aggressive transformation of the US energy industry over the next fifteen to twenty years to mitigate this catastrophic risk?

Helleurrrrrrrrrrrrrrrrrrrrrrrrrrrrrrrrr (Tyler Perry—HELLO)

Helleurrrrrrrrrrrrrrrrrrrrrrrrrrrrrrrrr

Let's answer a question with a question. Make sense? Let's see . . .

Why did the legalized slavery of African immigrants only last for 250 years in America?

Why did legalized segregation and discrimination of African immigrants only last for 100 years following slavery in America?

Let's go grab that definition of "unaccounted-for moral hazards" and reflect on that definition for a moment to capture the full context of what is happening here at this very important moment in American economic history. (I'm referring to the early 1950s.)

Definition: Unaccounted-for moral hazard

People or groups of people who exploit others outside their group to gain excessive wealth, power and control or to protect and keep excessive levels of wealth, power, and control at the expense of or even destruction of others outside their group eventually become so lustfully addicted to this exploitative behavior that when they have sucked all the exploitative juices out of the other group, they will turn this exploitative behavior on their own group, themselves—in effect, they become willing to "eat on" (exploit) members of their own group to satisfy their lust for increased wealth, power and control or to prevent losing massive levels of wealth, power and control previously obtained through exploitation.

Now let's ask the question, again, with unaccounted-for moral hazards as the contextual backdrop: Would there be any conceivable reason why the American energy industry, its associated businesses, and political and government leaders would not want to lead and inform the American public about the catastrophic risks associated with the predicted peak oil and natural gas production in the US by 1970 and the urgent need for an aggressive transformation of the US energy industry over the next fifteen to twenty years to mitigate this catastrophic risk to the US economy?

Let's see . . .

Potential reasons these groups may not have wanted to warn the American public about these catastrophic risks:

1. The high cost to the oil and natural gas industry of trying to discover, mine and produce new domestic supplies of oil and natural gas to mitigate the expected risk of peak and then declining oil and natural gas supplies expected in America by 1970.

2. The high cost to other energy industry suppliers of trying to discover alternative forms of energy at the quantity, quality and frequency needed to mitigate the risks of peak oil and natural gas production beginning in 1970.

3. The high opportunity cost to US industries and businesses if the US economy was purposely slowed down or made to ration consumption as was done during World War II, to "reduce" economic growth levels consistent with the predicted reduction in oil and natural gas production expected by 1970.

4. The massively high opportunity costs to the oil and natural gas industry of not having the opportunity to sell oil and natural gas supplies to the American public **at super high crazy, monopolistic, hostage price levels**, raking in massively crazy profits from these sales over many decades into the future . . . The opportunity to achieve these massively crazy profits for decades into the future *would be lost if the oil and gas industry actually figured out a way to increase oil and gas production by 1970*.

So, we can see that there were many reasons why the public might have been purposely left in the dark about rallying together to mitigate the catastrophic risk to the US economy of the predicted peak in US oil and natural gas supplies in the next fifteen to twenty years. Points 3 and 4 above are the most heinous and exploitative reasons for not informing the American public and show the cancerous impact cumulative unaccounted-for moral hazards have on the moral economic decision-making of leaders in America when "we" do not hold ourselves or our leadership into account.

So what happened between 1950 and 1970? Did America do the right thing? Did America:

1. Discover new ways to produce oil and natural gas?

2. Create alternative sources of energy to replace or support oil and natural gas production, sufficient to keep up with growth in the economy if oil and natural gas peaked in 1970?

3. Did the energy industry and business work with the government and the public to figure out how to slow economic growth down to levels consistent with our nation's energy supply capacity levels, preventing the economy from severely overheating, causing permanent damage to the US economy?

The answer to all these questions: NO, NO and HELL TO THE NO!

A nation that purposely ignores and does not learn from its history is tragically doomed to repeat its history and suffer more catastrophically because of its deliberate ignoring of history.

But oh! Wait a minute! What da . . . ? All this sounds eerily familiar!

Today, we are being warned about climate change. We see evidence of climate change affecting our environment and economy more and more heavily each year as we approach the year 2050, about twenty-five years from now, when America and the world need to reduce CO_2 emissions to zero, or irreparable damage and destruction associated with climate change will destroy life on this planet for all future generations.

But even though we see evidence of this plainly with the record temperature levels reached each year, flooding, droughts, hurricanes, wildfires and other natural disasters and pandemics, which are consistent with the predictions of the worst effects of climate change on course to occur if we do not make dramatic changes in decarbonizing our society and our economy over the next twenty-five years, a Pew Research Study shows that only 66% of Americans believe that the impacts of climate change will get materially worse from where we are today as we move into the future. WOW, the dilemma that we are dealing with in climate change today is an unaccounted for moral hazard. We have been here before. In the early 1950s. Let's go back to the tragic dilemma America was facing in the early 1950s and see what decisions were made.

Now, going back to the pending, so-called energy shortage that all the so-called experts were warning the US energy industry about in the early 1950s, twenty years before the shortage would occur, providing America and Americans plenty of time to prepare and adapt if the predictions turned out to be true.

What did America do?

Spoiled (unaccounted for moral hazards from slavery, segregation and discrimination) by not being held accountable for its previous, massive, economy-changing decisions, the business and energy industry fought tooth and nail against having to work collectively together as a country to avoid the energy shortage predicted by experts. The principal issue was that the energy industry, business and political interests did not want to fund this massive undertaking and essentially preached to the public that everything would be OK, would work itself out, we are America, the greatest economy in the world, we'll figure it out if the energy shortage happens, which was not 100% guaranteed. Scientists make predictions and estimates all the time. They're not always right, right? Why should we waste our time with massive new investments, transforming our energy system, when we don't know for sure that there will be an oil and natural gas energy supply crisis in America starting around 1970, right?

Again, this was a form of moral hazard or exploitation, but this time, the exploitation was not only of African Americans. The exploitation was of all of the American people, needlessly and preventable over the twenty-year period when the energy shortage was first identified. But the energy industry was in no panic. Why? Because if the cost of energy skyrocketed not just for a week, not just a month or a year or couple of years, but skyrocketed and stayed high for decades, who stood to make the most money from a sustained multi-decade occurrence like that? Yep, the energy industry. Let me hear it now: MORAL HAZARD!

The energy industry could have led a revolution to change the energy landscape in America with the help of the US government and still have been hugely profitable with good business on a sustainable basis going forward, but . . . but . . . but . . . but . . . if they sat back and did nothing and oil and natural gas supplies truly peaked in 1970, causing energy prices to soar and remain super high for many decades into the future, who in America would benefit most from that outcome? THE U.S. ENERGY INDUSTRY!

So let me ask you one more time. What do you think happened over the twenty-year period between 1950 and 1970 when America and the US energy industry had time to educate, invest and be prepared to have alternative energy supplies available if the worst case occurred and US energy scientists and economists were correct in predicting that US oil and gas supplies would peak in 1970?

CLOSE YOUR EYES, THINK, THINK ABOUT AMERICAN HISTORY AND AMERICAN BEHAVIOR BEFORE THIS PERIOD AND ANSWER THIS QUESTION YOURSELF: WHAT DO YOU THINK HAPPENED AND WHY? DID AMERICA STEP UP AND MEET ITS ENERGY SHORTAGE PROBLEM WITH NEARLY TWENTY YEARS TO PREPARE FOR IT? AND IF THEY DID OR DID NOT, WHY DID THEY BEHAVE THE WAY THEY DID?

In general, the public had little knowledge of the pending energy shortage or was not told the whole, clear truth about the implications and horribly catastrophic consequences for the US economy, if US energy industry scientists' and economists' predictions about US oil and natural gas supplies actually became true with US oil and natural gas supplies peaking by 1970, the very life blood of the US economy.

The energy industry, because of its underlying profit motive (separated and disconnected from morality, which, as we have discussed, is a structural problem in the US economy), had no real incentive to lead the effort of creating entirely new forms of energy to power America's economy. Here we see the problem again: economics separated from morality. The energy industry, seeing and understanding the huge and lasting catastrophic negative economic consequences of failing to solve an American oil and natural gas energy shortage, remained essentially silent about this massively important issue and downplayed and wrote off as extreme the views of those in the industry who suggested that the projected and expected peak in oil and natural gas production by 1970 was true or had any real likelihood of occurring.

__But this was exactly what happened! In 1970__, oil and natural gas production in America did peak and went into decline for the next forty years. For the first time in American history, the American economy was short of energy supplies needed to run the largest, most productive and most powerful economy on the planet. Energy supplies and energy prices are the most fundamental elements of an economy, especially the US economy.

Over the next thirteen years, from 1970 to 1983, energy prices in America increased by 1900% (crude oil was $2/bl in 1970 and skyrocketed to $40/bl by the early 1980s), creating what economists called the "Great Inflation" of the 1970s.

Because energy supplies and prices are the most fundamental and basic cost input to the US economy, the catastrophically high and sustained cost of energy in the US economy from 1970 to the early 1980s broke the economic backbone of the US economy over that thirteen-year period. By the early 1980s, the US economy had been so damaged by the sustained and catastrophically high cost of energy that it had actually become fundamentally and structurally uneconomic and began to need to borrow from other countries to stay afloat.

Because of the severity of the cost increases that took place in 1970 and were sustained over a thirteen-year period, many of the resources, tools and ways that the US economy used to work together to create profit and value added for consumers and business were now structurally, possibly permanently, broken and would require massive investments and cooperation by the American people to fix it.

But to really fix or repair the US economy and make it economic again, the business, financial and political establishment would have to admit what really happened to cause this massive economic calamity to disable and break the most powerful economic engine the world has ever known.

The energy industry and corporate America would have to admit they did nothing to seriously promote a solution to help prevent the energy shortage from occurring because they knew if oil and natural gas production actually peaked in 1970, as energy scientists and economists had predicted, the energy industry would actually reap the huge benefits of that outcome, even though it would be a catastrophe for the US economy and the American people as a whole. Again: ***unaccounted-for moral hazards***.

When you hear people talk about the great American decline, they are talking about when America began to lose its great inner cities, booming with factories, industrial work with great employment levels, companies making enough money to fund worker retirements and build and maintain good relationships with unions.

These people remember when good inner-city jobs supported the tax base of cities, where the difference between public and private schools was not that great in terms of the quality of education that American children received, and the cost of a home, a car, a college education or a vacation was much more affordable. The structural decline in the US economy all started in the 1980s following the thirteen-year Great Inflation of the 1970s, all because of the US energy industry's unaccounted-for moral hazards between 1950 and 1970.

Did you see what happened here? The insidiousness of habitual, unaccounted-for cumulative moral hazards, starting with slavery in this country, had become so acceptable, so seductive and so enticing and delicious that an industry and political establishment that had so faithfully served America over the course of America's history fell prey to the temptation of taking the path of least resistance, deciding not to actively promote the catastrophic seriousness of the energy shortage challenge forecasted to take place in 1970.

As we discussed earlier, one of the most evil characteristics or qualities of unaccounted-for cumulative moral hazards is that, when the wealthy and powerful exploiting group can no longer exploit "others" or "them" who are outside the exploiting group, the exploiting group will begin to exploit itself or exploit members of its own group to reap the excessively attractive profits, wealth and power for the privileged few in its group, now at the expense and catastrophic destruction of "not just African Americans," but now willing to heap this exploitation on good old red-blooded, white, loyal, Christian and patriotic military American veterans, etc. They are willing now to eat their own to protect the benefits of past or gains from future expected exploitive behaviors.

The exploiting group may now try to wrap the purpose of the exploitative behavior around issues of race, sexual preference, crime, immigration, abortion, etc. Now that they are eating their own, they need to make a justified excuse for the exploitive behavior that is now clearly immoral, but by wrapping it up in an ideology or conspiracy theory, they can make their immoral actions, through lies and distortions, moral again. If you ask the question why behind all of these phony excuses or reasons behind why there is such a fervent ideological drive to support the destruction of things very useful institutions in society, like public schools, Diversity, Equity and Inclusion programs, the Environmental Protection Agency, Welfare, Social Security, Federal Support for Health Care, the Federal Reserve, Food, Health and Safety Regulations, Federal Disaster

Protection Agencies, etc., the underlying reason that these great and necessary institutions are being lobbied to get rid of is for the following reasons:

1. The exploiting group does not want to pay any taxes or higher taxes or the increased cost of making society and the economy work best for everyone.

2. The exploiting group desires to capitalize on an opportunity that will bring the exploiting group massive profits, wealth, power and control, but only if "others" or "them" (US middle and lower income) are sacrificed or even destroyed in the process. Win by any means possible. If you lose in the competition, too bad. ***Get out the way, die and move over and let the winners thrive and have a NICE DAY!*** Even if the way that they won (exploiters) is unfair and immoral, get over it. Life is unfair. Less people to worry about, less food and energy needed to take care of the winners who have survived. This is reality and this is life, even though it is not the nice little fairy tale we taught you about life and morality when you were growing up as a child.

Moral hazard is economic development that takes the "we," "us" and morality out of economic decision-making and happily and aggressively brings in the concept of "us vs. them," where the "them" are the bad, the evil, the undeserving or simply the different and therefore the "us" does not have to consider, worry about, protect or include "them" in their economic considerations.

The problem is that unchecked cumulative moral hazard has no loyalty, no empathy and no heart and will eventually exploit and consume even itself, not seeing that it is eating itself to death, because it is so focused on winning the exploitation game by any means possible.

Let's recap.

We are now in the early 1980s. The US economy is in a deep recession resulting from thirteen years of roaring energy prices, which have literally broken and beaten down the US economy, such that the US economy is actually no longer economic.

Such a tragedy: the greatest economic engine the world has ever experienced, destroyed by its own choosing, by its own people and institutions. But this is what happens when economic moral hazards are allowed to persist in the economy without being held to account. These behaviors will be repeated with greater negative impact for a wider range of people in the group and in the economy. Slavery, segregation and discrimination have and continue to negatively impact African-Americans in America to this day. The moral hazards associated with America's first national energy crisis broke the competitive economic backbone of the world's greatest economy, transforming it into a debt-addicted financial and political system with absolutely no morality—setting the stage for the significant and increased structural division, chaos and polarization in the US economy from the 1980s to this day.

So what should America do now to deal with its economy, which for the first time in its history is now structurally uneconomic, unable to grow without suffering losses and causing the US economy to turn even more negative with the passage of time?

Should America do the right thing, slow its economy down, take time to rebuild and structure itself so that it is fundamentally economic again?

Or should America take the quick path of least resistance, not learning from its past two great moral hazards—slavery and the first energy crisis—and decide to do a quick fix to the US economy, which really does not fix it but instead simply hides the losses it's creating, making it look like the US economy is healthy and growing?

So what did America do at this third major decision point in US economic history in the early 1980s? (Following the Great Inflation of the 1970s, caused by America not fixing its oil and natural gas shortage problem, identified in the early 1950s, that gave America ample time to prepare for solving the oil and gas energy shortage predicted to occur in 1970, but America decided not to prepare for it, giving us the Great Inflation of the 1970s.)

Unfortunately, and as you might expect by now, given the economic decisions that America has made up to this point in its history, America once again decided to take the path of least resistance, deciding to again exploit the middle and working class in America.

Again, America could have chosen to do the right thing—business, industry and government coming together to structurally fix the high-cost uneconomic drivers in the US economy related to energy, materials and manufacturing, which would have taken time but would have put the US economy on a healthy and strong fundamental economic course to rebuild and become an even stronger and better and more sustainable leader in the global economy.

However, that was not America's choice. America chose to follow the path of least resistance—the Reagan Revolution, low taxes, limited government and financial engineering as the secret sauce for restoring economic greatness to America (not all of America and not all Americans but primarily the top 10%–20% of Americans as it relates to accumulated wealth).

But again, as we discussed above, low taxes, financial engineering and selling American industry and jobs to emerging market economies is a revolution, a revolution to consolidate power, wealth and control of the US economy increasingly in the hands of the much richer few at the top and at the expense and detriment of everyone else, creating a lack of control, much less wealth and much more chaos and polarization for the bottom 80% of Americans in America.

Financial engineering was another gimmick, a con game to put off doing the hard, smart and innovative work required to transform and make the US economy fundamentally and structurally lowest cost again, with actual and real superior affordability to US consumers and the lowest cost of doing business for manufacturing and service industries on the planet.

After failing to address the moral hazards of slavery and the first energy crisis, you would have thought that America would have learned its lesson by now and chosen to do the hard, smart and moral work required to fix the US economy and make it economic, working best for everyone in the US, and not artificially rigging it to work best for the wealthiest and well connected, RIGHT?

But actually, the converse is what happened. Since America never addressed its moral hazards associated with slavery and the first energy crisis, what the law of moral hazards suggests is that cumulative unchecked moral hazards incentivize people or groups to continue exploiting moral hazards in the future because they have and continue to get away with not being held accountable.

Again, as Tyler Perry would say, Helleurrrrrrrrrrrrrrrrrrr!

So actually it makes perfect sense that America was fully on board with the Reagan Revolution, the financialization and transformation of the economy into a Ponzi Scheme Financial System.

Beginning in 1983, America started using financial engineering to artificially grow the US economy with uneconomic financial activity disguised as real fundamental economic activity. This financial engineering allowed America's broken and super high-cost economy to borrow and finance the super high cost of living in America and the super high cost of doing business in America, with the ability to hide and park those loan and liability obligations somewhere in the US or global financial system, making it appear that those debts/obligations were for all practical purposes not there. Thus, in the near to medium term (next 10–20 years), the US economy was made to look healthy, strong and able to fully and competitively support its overpriced, high-cost economy, which was actually leveraged up to its nose.

The following five economic and financial indicators help us assess vulnerabilities and structural weaknesses in the US economy:

1. US velocity of money

2. US public and private sector debt levels as a percentage of GDP

3. US current account deficit

4. Credit default swaps on US treasuries

5. America's confidence in Congress's ability to pass and enforce sufficient and sustainable national budgets

Inspection and review of these five economic and financial indicators show clearly that the US economy is not economical but is really a financial system where the majority of the wealth in America is consolidated in the top 1%–5% of the population, while the economy for the bottom 80%–90% is unaffordable and does not work best, but increasingly works against them because of the excessively high cost of living and the high cost of doing business. If you have massive amounts of wealth, then of course you are not hampered by the high cost of living or the high cost of doing business in America. But how many Americans have this luxury? (about 30–40 million, but what about the other 290 million Americans? Uh what about them? America's current value system appears to be moving increasingly toward the view that if you lost, for whatever reason, even if you were downright cheated, too bad, move over, die and get the hell out the way, so the winners can thrive and continue to have a nice day!)

The decision to financialize the US economy was a structural vote against the belief that the American workforce had and has the will, creativity and ability to work with the US government and corporate America to repair, fix and upgrade the US economy to be the best and lowest cost economy on the planet.

The financialization of the US economy also made it very easy for large American companies and corporations to sell their businesses to foreign companies, to offshore jobs and set up companies in foreign countries where employment pay was just a fraction of the cost in America.

This is exactly why America and the bottom 80% of Americans felt a very real decline, loss of wealth, loss of control and loss of buying power from the 1980s to 2008, because that is exactly what happened. The laws were set up to incentivize corporations to offshore jobs overseas and allow the wealthiest Americans to benefit most significantly by selling their assets in America and investing internationally where US corporations were investing and setting up shop to manufacture in these countries and then ship products and services back to America.

These laws, tax breaks and incentives made corporations and wealthy investors excessively wealthy at the direct expense and

destruction of income and opportunities for the bottom 80% of Americans in America. This was done because conservative wealth and power holders in this country did not want to admit that the economy was broken and high cost, because conservative business interests had not wanted to invest in the US energy industry back in the 1950s to prevent the Great Inflation from occurring. Additionally, the conservative movement did not want to fix the US economy and make it competitive and economic in the early 1980s, after the Great Inflation broke the economic backbone of the economy, preferring rather to sell off America's great industries and jobs to the international community, making US corporations and investors new millionaires and billionaires on the backs of lost jobs, lost industries, lost American expertise, lost homes, lost communities and devastated inner cities for middle- and working-class Americans all over America, the bottom 80% of the American population.

This was a conscious, deliberate and direct exploitation of the American people by the Reagan Revolution and the Republican Party.

From 1980 to 2008, when America started operating its Ponzi Scheme economy for the rich, the overwhelming majority of Americans saw their spending power decline by 90%, while the wealthy and the well-connected saw their wealth grow by about 150% over the same period.

Over this twenty-five-year period, financial and economic experts painted a picture showing the success of raw and brutal capitalism, suggesting that America's Ponzi Scheme economy was really healthy and strong by pointing to the extreme wealth created by the winners in the economy and trying by association to suggest that all of America and all Americans were enjoying the same success.

But most Americans over this twenty-five-year period were losing jobs, losing retirement benefits, losing healthcare benefits, losing full-time employment benefits, unable to save sufficiently (or at all) for retirement, unable to pay for their own education or their children's education or taking out loans to pay for education and healthcare, which affected their financial positions for the rest of their lives. No spare saving for family vacations, maybe one to two vacations over the life of the family versus wealthy families in the US economy benefiting from a financial system that excessively rewarded the wealthy and well connected, who were able to enjoy a nice vacation three to six times a year.

Conservative policies of excessively low taxes and limited government are the very reasons America *has not invested in itself.* And because of this, the cost of living and doing business in America is uncompetitively too high. Government spending to help poor and working-class Americans with the cost of living is at an all-time high, but that is not because government is bad, wasteful and unnecessary. The only reason the government is providing this support is because the market prices that the US Ponzi Scheme economy charges for goods and services are too expensive for normal working Americans. The historical cause of these excessively high unaffordable market prices is *perfectly explained* by the wealthy conservative business interest's failure to support investing in the energy industry in the twenty years leading up to the Great Inflation of the 1970s and their failure to invest in repairing and fundamentally fixing the uncompetitive high costs of the US economy broken during the Great Inflation.

The largest and most sustained tax cuts in American history were implemented during the Reagan, Bush and Trump administrations. Those $20 to $40 trillion in tax breaks could have easily paid for the investments in the energy, industry, education and healthcare industries, making the market cost of living and the market cost of doing business in America globally competitive, keeping industries and jobs in America, with products, services and retirement savings affordable and competitive, without the need for the excessive government support that is provided by governments today, not because people are lazy and do not want to work but because the market costs for vital products and services in the US economy are unaffordable for the overwhelming majority of US consumers.

Conservatives' revolutionary call for limited government and low taxes is antithetical to the US Preamble and the Constitution of the United States. The Constitution implores all Americans to actively and collectively work together as much as possible to create win-win solutions for our economy that will in turn make the country work best for all Americans, both individually and collectively, synergistically and most productively sharing our resources, time, efforts and creativities to make this happen.

Low taxes and limited government is just another way of saying, "I'm successful. I got mines. I like the way things are. I don't want or need things to change, because I want to keep what I have and keep the advantages that I have, and if others in America are having problems or need help, that's their problem. I got mine, so they have to figure a way to get theirs. Not my problem." That is not what the Constitution implies, and that view explains precisely why America's costs are so high and its debts are the highest in the global economy. We are the United States of America, not the "I Got Mine" States of America.

The 2007–9 Global Credit Crisis and Great Recession was the actual recognition that the great US economy, created during the

Reagan Revolution, was really a fake Ponzi Scheme economy, that is, a financial system, not an economy, rigged to make the rich much richer at the expense and destruction of the way of life, wealth and wellbeing of the overwhelming majority of Americans, the bottom 80%.

From 1983 to 2007, the US economy was operating like a rigged financial system and not a competitive economy based on strong economic fundamentals from the bottom up. Again, in the early 1980s, America had an opportunity to slow down and work toward creating a fundamentally and structurally strong economy based on bottom up strong economic fundamentals, but America decided that it would be easier to leave the economy broken, fundamentally too expensive, and just use financial engineering to grow it uneconomically by borrowing from other countries and itself to pay for the high cost of living and the high cost doing business, hiding that borrowing and those losses in the financial system until . . . until . . . until the borrowing and losses had built up to such high levels that they could no longer be hidden and contained in the elaborate Ponzi Scheme financial system that America had created for itself because it did not want to put in the work and creativity required to fix and make the economy fundamentally economic, strong and sustainable for all of the American people, back in the early 1980s.

The 2007–9 Global Credit Crisis and Great Recession was America's Ponzi Scheme financial system trying to go bankrupt, and it would have gone bankrupt if the US government and the global banking system hadn't doubled down and effectively done what it had done over the previous twenty-five years, borrowing more money from other countries and from the US itself to provide $10–$15 trillion in loans to once again finance uneconomic growth in the US and global economy from 2009 until today.

If America does not take the time to convert its Ponzi Scheme financial system back into a healthy and productive economic economy, sooner or later it will implode, creating permanent and unrecoverable losses for everyone, the rich and the poor alike. Remember, in a Ponze Scheme, eventually, everyone loses, not just the dumb, exploited suckers represented by the masses, but the dumb suckers at the top, who actually knew/know that the day of reckoning was coming, but they were/are enjoying their temporary benefits while they can, even though this means that their children, grandchildren and all future generations of Americans' lives will be permanently ruined for their temporary period of excessive pleasure and joy.

Did you see what happened after the 2007–9 Global Credit Crisis and Great Recession? Did America finally learn its lesson after running the US economy like a Ponzi scheme from 1983 to 2008, exploiting the bottom 80% of all Americans so that the top 20% could grow and become excessively wealthy at the expense of and even destruction of the bottom 80% of Americans in America, while also almost destroying the global financial system in the process?

No, no, no, and HELL TO THE NO. And America has still not learned its lesson.

But again, this should come as no surprise. It is so much easier to double down and just finance all the losses from the Global Credit Crisis and Great Recession on the Central Bank's balance sheet and again spread out these losses conveniently across the global financial system and continue the bigger and broader financialization of the US and global economies, aggressively creating much more wealth, power and control for the top 1–10%, increasingly at the expense and destruction of the bottom 80%, because the financial system does not have a soul or social evaluation criteria to see how its profit motive impacts people, the environment, safety, health, quality of life, etc.

Those with wealth and income in the top 10%–20% attempt to create a narrative that this process is healthy for everyone in the financial system and that the great success they are experiencing and enjoying is actually being fairly and equally shared and felt by the entire public. The ultimate exploitation though that keeps this con game for the extremely wealthy and powerful is that they create the ultimate conspiracy theory, which they sell to the bottom 80%, which is really perversely against the bottom 80%'s economic and financial interest, and 100% to the benefit of the wealthiest 10% in the US and global economy. I discussed this previously, but I repeat it here again:

The con game goes like this:

1. The federal government is the source of all of the economy's problems because the government seeks to help and include everyone, and in the process of doing that, it has to borrow massive amounts of money, and that is why our economy is so expensive and unaffordable.

2. We should have limited government and the lowest amount of taxes possible. Actually, no taxes would be perfect, because for almost everything we need, the free market does a much better job of managing the economy; it's only when governments get involved that money gets wasted. Government never achieves what it sets out to accomplish and wastes so much time trying to.

3. Including everyone and worrying about whether everyone is being treated justly and fairly is too expensive and is a form

of socialism or communism, which never works and causes economies to go broke.

As we have seen over the course of actual US economic history and based on what the words in the Constitution actually say and mean:

1. The reason the US and global economy is so expensive for the bottom 80% is because the top 10% have not and do not want to work with the rest of the population to structurally fix the broken, uneconomic elements in the economy because they are doing fine keeping things just like they are. If the economy were actually corrected to work best for everyone, the top 10% would not be able to exploit others and create wealth for themselves as easily and quickly as they have done in the past and as they are able to do today. These conditions make products and services so expensive that the bottom 80% have to continually borrow massively more amounts of debt and nearly bankrupt themselves to afford essential products and services in life (housing, healthcare, transportation, education, insurance, retirement, etc.). The top 10% benefits wildly from this because . . .

2. The very rich and wealthy actually do not want to fix the structurally high cost of living and the structurally high cost of doing business in the economy because they make so much more money by keeping the economy broken and unproductive *because they can charge higher and higher prices on goods and services with the passage of time and continue to loan more consumers bigger and bigger loans to pay for the higher and higher costs of the products and services that they need to buy from the top 10%.*

This is how and why I call the financial system that was created and expanded into the global economy under Reagan in the early 1980s to this day a ***Ponzi Scheme financial system***, one that is rigged to make the rich richer and everyone else poorer or bankrupt over time. Again, the problem with this approach is that eventually everyone loses, rich and poor alike, because this system automatically creates an economic cancer in the core of its system that is guaranteed to metastasize and become malignant, destroying the financial system for everyone, right before our blinded but wide-open eyes.

This fate is not the inevitable end, however.

The Economic Gospel for the USA is about repairing, fixing and upgrading the broken parts of the US economy so that the economy becomes economic again, not needing to eat itself to grow and prosper, but rather regenerate and create new life and resources which grow the pie of life, creating abundance, spare capacity and balance that will give life and the economy plenty of room to grow and prosper on a sustainable basis going forward, in ways that benefit all, for all, rather than massively benefitting the few through the egregious and destructive exploitations of the many. The Economic Gospel for the USA and the US Preamble give us the perfect formula for creating and maintaining this for America and the world. I will spell out this formula in detail toward the end of this book.

••

UKRAINE

"Until a man has found something that he is willing to die for, he isn't fit to live." — Martin Luther King, Jr.

America and Europe absolutely have the power, influence and moral support of the world and history to forcefully, boots on the ground, assist Ukraine in defending its people and its sovereignty from an evil and forceful domination by Russia.

All diplomatic avenues have been pursued. Defending democracy, truth and morality does not mean defending only by non-violent and non-forceful actions. When all diplomatic options have been exhausted, violence and force may very well be required to win the war between good and evil and between truth and lies. Light and darkness cannot coexist in the same space in time.

Light in this context is the support, promotion and development of human life on this planet, where people are free to learn, work and play together in ways that create maximum opportunities for everyone in society to have the best chance of developing into the best possible versions of themselves. Darkness in this context is every and any process that attempts to dim or put out that light, destroying people's ability and opportunities to become the best possible versions of themselves. Unfortunately, failing to promote and defend good is an invitation for lies and evil to flourish, grow, gain power, and dominate. America and Europe's failure to promote and defend Ukraine by force, given Russia's lustful desire to deny Ukraine's right to exist as a free and independent nation, will be an invitation to Russia, China, North Korea and all other dark actors on the planet to unite and pull the trajectory of human history down into a dark, tragic and destructive end.

America and Europe's failure to defend Ukraine will also invite tens of millions of Ukrainian citizens to lose faith and allegiance with democracy, truth and the good, seeing these ideologies as weak and only supportive of those with wealth and influence, no better than dictatorships when it comes down to it.

I am not better than Putin; none of us are. But Putin's mind and spirit are sick and a cancer on life and morality. His sick views and conspiracy theories on life are twisted to justify his lust for power and control and the absolute destruction and killing of innocent people. The lessons of World War II have taught us that we cannot fear or back down from evil because its unquenchable lust for exceedingly more power and control will not stop unless it is put down.

Putin is acting on his most negative ambitions with force. We must meet force with force when there is no alternative for protecting love, truth, justice, respect and honor for human life on this planet. Ultimately, however, we must heal the broken hearts, minds and spirits of the Russian people, who are the ultimate source of Putin's power. The solution for this is presented at the end of this book.

••

GLOBAL PANDEMICS

From the very start of the pandemic, American leadership used Covid-19 as an opportunity to divide, create lies, hate, distortion and polarization, solely for the purposes of political and economic gain, but at the direct expense and unnecessary killing of more Americans in *just two years* than all the Americans killed in all of its wars since and including the Civil War.

This unnecessary polarization forced America to also spend $10 trillion to save the US and world economy from economic collapse, precisely because Americans would not be American to one another.

This $10 trillion in debt will be on the backs of current and future generations of Americans for many generations into the future. America, the wealthiest, most powerful and most scientifically and medically sophisticated country on the planet, has had the absolute worst response to Covid-19 on the planet, with by far the most cases and most people unnecessarily killed than any other country by an extremely large margin.

This catastrophic killing spree and catastrophically massive debt load addition to America's balance sheet was almost entirely preventable if Americans had just been American to each other as defined in the Preamble to the Constitution.

Remember former President Obama and the Ebola outbreak? Obama's non-controversial resolution to that global crisis (which could have turned into a far worse deadlier global outbreak than Covid-19, given the much deadlier nature and contagiousness of the Ebola virus, to all age levels) *was to lead with science and public safety as the highest priority*, maintaining secure and friendly diplomatic relations with the countries that were the source of the outbreak, working together to contain the outbreak in those countries to the greatest degree possible, with scientists leading the national and global discussion to ensure that public opinion was, to the greatest degree possible, all on the same page rooted in facts and history easily verified by everyone.

In May 2018, former President Trump disbanded the Global Health Security and Biodefense unit—responsible for pandemic preparedness—that had been established in 2015 by Obama's National Security Advisor, Susan Rice. The unit, which resided under the National Security Council (NSC), had been created to maintain the continuity of lessons learned and successes achieved in combating global pandemics and to use that knowledge and experience to minimize the confusion, harm and deaths that might result from future pandemics.

This disbandment and elimination of funding for a coordinated response from the executive office of the US government was a deliberate strategic decision and failure by the Trump administration, ignoring the importance of successful lessons learned by the US government in successfully fighting global pandemics from the very recent past, and left the Trump administration totally unprepared and the American population totally exposed when the Covid-19 virus began to spread globally in October–November of 2019.

This was another clear example of a catastrophic unaccounted for economic moral hazard in America by the Republican Party led by former President Trump. Former President Trump despised everything and anything to do with Former President Obama as evidenced by his many statements and actions both before and after Obama became President. (See, for instance, the conspiracy theory campaign he led for many years before and during Obama's presidency, claiming that former President Obama was not a citizen of the United States, many years after both he and the public had been shown proof of Obama's official citizenship status.) Upon becoming president, former President Trump was therefore on a mission to purge or reverse as many policies and actions that even remotely looked or smelled like they originated from the Obama administration, even if those policies were good, well-structured and necessary for the safety and protection of the American people.

Former President Trump's disbanding of the Global Health Security and Biodefense unit was an act of pure hubris and narcissism, emboldening former President Trump's feeling and beliefs of absolute power and control, which blinded former President Trump from seeing the value of the unit as a safety net for his administration and a safety net for the American people. The disbanding of the unit by former President Trump destroyed his administration's capacity to effectively respond to Covid-19 when it began to spread across the globe in the fourth quarter of 2019, resulting in:

1. Over one million Americans unnecessarily killed over two years because of Trump's unpreparedness and outright failure to lead with the science like all other countries did who were successful in containing the spread of Covid-19, even before a vaccine was discovered. The real tragedy is that former President Trump did show leadership, but his leadership was manipulative and evil, spreading lies, conspiracy theories and chaos. The buck stops the top: Former Trump is directly responsible for the unnecessary killing of a million Americans over two years.

2. The $10 million in debt that the US government had to spend to save the economy from collapse related to the pandemic during 2020–21 was all directly a result of former President Trump's decisions to disband and dismantle the government structures built up over many years to be prepared to protect the American public specifically from global pandemics like Covid-19.

3. Former President Trump's leadership of chaos and lies, specifically for the purpose of dividing the country, using the pandemic as a tool to get more of the American people to follow and support his candidacy for reelection by making it a badge of honor and a sign of patriotic freedom and true Americanism if you rejected science, common sense, and any

established norms for protecting one's self from respiratory viruses that the world has known and used for centuries.

Former President Trump preached a gospel of "rejecting anything that science and people in authority have to say about keeping yourself safe from respiratory viruses" . . . except, of course, for advice that he would provide. As the former president has preached many times, only he, Donald Trump, has the wisdom, knowledge and experience that the public should trust and put our faith in. We see the same kind of self-protecting manipulative falsehoods in the movement against wokeness, because wokeness threatens to reveal former President Trump's lies for what they are.

4. *The roaring and high inflation levels in the economy, which persist to this day, and the unnecessary deaths of more than one million Americans in only two years are directly and causally related to former President Trump's policies and decision framework.* Because of the disbandment of the Global Health Security/Biodefense unit and Trump's harsh and uneconomic trade policies with China, America was caught off guard, totally naked and unprepared and did not have the capacity to work hand in glove with China to mitigate the worst effects of Covid-19 on the front end of the pandemic, in China, where the virus originated from, as the Obama administration had successfully done in the case of the much more deadly and much more contagious Ebola virus. Studies were completed early in 2019 in the global medical community warning of the risk of a virus like Covid-19 pandemic originating in China, and these studies were completely ignored by the Trump administration, or worse yet, the studies were available and we did not know they were there

to study, learn from and prepare for because we recklessly disbanded our planning processes that would have prepared us to look for and act on studies like this. Had America been working more closely together with other countries, as we had prior to Trump's abrasive and uneconomic trade policies and dismantling of the Global Health Security and Biodefense unit, a great deal of the social and economic damage caused by the Covid-19 pandemic could have been totally prevented, including the excessive and catastrophic rise in inflation over the past 4 years.

Thus, America's response to Covid-19, the absolute worst on the planet, from the country that had been the most successful in fighting and leading the world in containing global pandemics, was a massive failure during the Covid-19 pandemic because of the Trump Administration's gutting of the executive office's Pandemic Preparedness Unit and total politicization of the Pandemic Response process, which should have been led by the science, as was successfully done during the Obama administration for the H1N1 and Ebola pandemics of 2009 and 2014, respectively.

Oh, and by the way, do you know what year the wealthiest Americans in America made the most money ever in one year? Approximately $20 trillion between 2020 and 2021, when the government released the funds that were supposed to go to the neediest of the needy, illustrating the massive exploitation and abuse of power available to the wealthiest and most well-connected in American society and the economy.

In these two years, more Americans were unnecessarily killed than all American soldiers killed in all American wars since and including the Civil War, because of the politicalization of Covid-19, and the wealthiest Americans in America increased their wealth by $20 trillion dollars, using government money to catastrophically enrich themselves, while America's economy experienced the sharpest and quickest downturn in American history.

The velocity of money in America plunged to all-time crazy record low levels during and following the Covid-19 pandemic, an outward demonstration of the egregious concentration of wealth in the US economy, indicating that the money supply is not efficiently and productively being dispersed throughout the economy for all Americans to use, creating better and the best opportunities for all Americans to benefit from and develop into the best possible versions of themselves.

The money supply and liquidity is concentrated in the hands of the wealthiest 10% of Americans in the economy who have the ability to use that wealth and liquidity to make America and especially its financial system work catastrophically much better for the top 10%, at the expense of the bottom 80% of middle-, working- and lower-income Americans, who make up the overwhelming majority of people in this country.

As we have discussed, the US economy has been structurally broken since the early 1980s. The lopsidedness and ability of the US economy to be rigged and slanted to so grossly work in the favor of the top 10% is the result of the economy remaining in its broken, unrepaired and uneconomic state over the past fifty years.

••

FORMER PRESIDENT DONALD TRUMP

The reason former president Donald Trump has the power to hijack the Republican Party is because he has infused into the Party a massive number of new members who he has conned into believing that only he, Donald Trump, sees their pain, only he sees how unfairly life is treating them, only he will fight and win by any means possible to get rid of and even destroy the Democrats or the traditional Republicans who have exploited and abused these new members of the Republican Party. Only Donald Trump will go to war for these new members and create opportunities for them to be wealthy, healthy and powerful like their great and fearless leader, Trump himself.

Former president Trump's supporters know and believe that he will cheat, lie, steal and kill to protect them and represent their interests. Problem is, that is what former president Trump promises, just to get their votes, but once he is in power, he has demonstrated that he will narcissistically do whatever he wants to do and will turn his back on his most loyal supporters in the blink of an eye without remorse. Former vice president Mike Pence is the ultimate example of this.

Many of former president Trump's followers are truly victims of the broken and exploitative US economy of the last fifty years that we have discussed in previous sections of this text. Many of them are also people who have not made the best choices in life and are looking for another option. The problem here is that Trump's life legacy demonstrates that he represents the epitome of the social and economic disease that has had its foot on the back of many of the Republican Party's new supporters. Trump is running the ultimate con game on the American people and most tragically on his newer, cult-like followers, whom he and America's financial system have exploited for the last fifty years, and is now coming to these same people and saying that he will be their savior.

Psychologically, it is a boost to the self-esteem or feelings of self-worth for these Trump supporters, because now they can say to themselves, "It's not my fault I didn't rise to the levels of success, fortune and power that I should have been able to achieve, because I've been unfairly held back by the lack of representation from Democrats and traditional Republicans.

Democrats and traditional Republicans are the enemy now; Trump is our savior."

Does former President Trump lie and cheat to win? Yes, and as a matter of fact, "HELL YES," but that's OK with Trump's new Republican supporters, who feel they have been lied to and cheated by the hypocritical Democrats and traditional Republicans all of their lives.

It's payback time now. They are for former president Trump, who will save them, get revenge for them and open the doors of opportunity to America for them, and yes! Former president Trump may do this by lying, cheating and even hurting and killing others along the way, but that's life in the big city. The real world is not perfect, and sometimes we need to just hire someone who will get the job done by any means possible.

And because Trump's supporters believe this about him, it is true that he can do just about any horrible or immoral thing he wants to do. That is what his followers really expect him to do. The crazier Trump's actions are, deep down in his followers' spirits—their souls cry out Yes and Halleluia because they believe he's willing to be crazy enough to represent and protect his supporters' interests no matter what!

The problem is, again, this is all a con game.

Former president Trump only ran for the presidency to use it as a shield to delay all of the criminal charges and indictments against him until he gets elected, and if he gets elected, he'll get the cases dismissed and attempt to turn America into an autocracy similar to what Russia is today, with the goal of remaining in office likely until he dies or gets laws passed that will allow him to be immune from criminal prosecution in any manner or fashion.

Former president Trump has shown us he has absolutely no loyalty to anyone. He will drop and crucify his most loyal followers if they do not follow his every command, even if following that command means breaking the law or putting you and your family's lives at risk. Again: former vice president Mike Pence. Do I need to go any further? Former president Trump's most loyal follower, who bent over backwards over the course of the Trump presidency, lying and ignoring many of his conservative principles to demonstrate his loyalty and commitment in front of the entire nation and the entire world, for four full years, and in the blink of an eye, Trump threw Mike Pence to the wolves on January 6th because he would not cooperate with the illegal insurrection on the United States of America.

Now if he will do this to his most loyal warrior, who was literally by his side and on his team for four years, what do you think he is going to do for his supporters once he gets in office and no longer needs his supporters to get what he wants? Actions speak much louder than words. Again, he threw his most loyal confidant under the bus for all the world to see, without any shame or remorse, knowing that he was asking Pence to break the law.

I know this seems kind of farfetched, but when you think about it, not really. Former president Donald Trump has been impeached twice, has 91 indictments against him, has a horrible business legacy of cheating those who he has done business with, and he is leading in the polls for the presidency of the United States of America in June of 2024, with the election only five months away.

But really, this is nothing new.

The Republican Party has been running a con game on the American people since the Reagan Revolution of the early 1980s, as discussed in the previous section.

Trump has just found a way to play on the sentiments and disappointments of Democrats and traditional Republican voters who feel they have been cheated in life and want someone to blame and demonize for their disappointments.

Trump plays on the disappointment, grief and low self-esteem of these supporters by lifting them up through victimization, showing them who their enemies are, and promising to exact revenge on them—the Democrats and traditional Republicans—as a means of liberating his new supporters because the process of exacting that revenge will open the doors to economic and financial opportunities for his new supporters. This is not true, and former president Trump does not have to explicitly promise this to many of them. These new supporters of Trump believe that they are on the Trump team and can show the Democrats and traditional Republican Party that their vote can no longer be taken for granted; their support for Trump is a middle finger to the Democrats and traditional Republicans. For many of them, just having the ability to show Democrats and Traditional Republicans that they do not need them and better yet will vote for the former president Trump no matter what intelligence, reports, information that is provided to them that shows them that voting for the former president Trump is not in their economic or social interest. Having the power to give the Democrats and the Traditional Republicans the middle finger is more than enough for them. Even if Trump gets elected and they find out that everything that they were warned about former president Trump is true, they will feel good in their souls that they had the power to give the Democrats and the Traditional Republicans the middle finger during the election.

Actually, former president Trump is not some strange once-in-a-century leader, freak of nature or enigma who has somehow come and miraculously taken over the Republican Party, such that now the Republican Party is a helpless victim of this evil, bad and mad man who has arrived on the body politic in America. No, Trump is actually the existential expression of the Republican Party incarnate, speaking out loud clearly and expressly for all of America and the world to see and understand, transparently, leaving little doubt about who he is and what his intentions are.

Outwardly, most Republicans will not behave or speak the way former president Trump does, but inwardly they are in lockstep with the former president. The primary reason for this is that the net result of former president Trump's policies is to basically preserve the status quo, or better yet, take us back to a previous status quo and ignore the structural economic and social challenges that will destroy America and the world, if we just close our eyes and assume that the free market will solve everything if we just "get the hell out of the way" and let life and business naturally unfold as it has done for the past fifty years.

Let me see, I think we heard this same view back in February of 2020, before Covid-19 had begun to spread catastrophically through-out America. At that time Trump was preaching the misinformation chaos gospel that Covid-19 was no more harmful than the common cold/flu—"Don't worry about it, everything is going to be OK, no need for massive government interventions and preparations, the existing market knows best and will handle everything, we are OK, it will all just go away."

Two years later, with one million Americans unnecessarily killed by Covid-19, America had to borrow $10 trillion, against itself, to save our economy from collapsing, and over that same period, the wealthiest top 10% of Americans increased their wealth by the largest amount in American history, $20 trillion, when the US economy was on its back. Fathom that! That sure does not sound like everything was just OK . . .

••

The Source of Inflation in the US Economy

The true sources of the excessive inflation in the US economy over the past four years can be explained perfectly by the very proactive and structural chaos-creating influences and policies of the former President Trump and his administration:

1. *Relations with Iran*

   President Trump nearly destroyed the Iranian economy and created tremendous chaos and insecurity in the Middle East and around the globe by pulling out of the US-negotiated nuclear agreement with Iran in 2017. This blatant political act of revenge by former President Trump to show his power and defiance of the previous administration demonstrates Trump's willingness to sacrifice the integrity and the commitments of the United States of America with our international partners for his own personal gains and demonstrations of power and control. The chaos and threats posed by Iran today are at near catastrophic levels compared to where they were before the nuclear deal was ended. With the deal, we had a trusted and reliable relationship building with Iran, with the threat of military escalation between Iran and our allies in the Middle East expected to stabilize and significantly improve going forward.

After being kicked to the curb by the US, nearly destroying the Iranian economy with massive sanctions following Trump's cancellation of the nuclear deal, Iran is now in full solidarity with Russia, China, and North Korea, willing and ready to destabilize and disrupt America and democracy on every front, because we, America, went back on our word to the Iranian people. How could they ever think about trusting America and its allies, either now or in the future, knowing that the next president could, at his own selfish whim, destroy any agreements that were made by the previous administration?

2. *Relations with China*

Former President Trump's malicious and uneconomic trade war with China: As we have discussed in this text, China is not our enemy. Between 1980 and 2008, America went to China looking for cheap labor and cheap resources to sell out American industries and jobs so that American and global investors could reap catastrophically enormous profits, at the direct expense and financial destruction of American industries, companies, and jobs.

China is not our enemy; they did not come looking to steal and take our industries, companies, and jobs; American international investors and corporations went to China willingly, looking for the fastest and easiest way to make the largest profits in human history over the past forty years, not for the American people, but for the super wealthy top 10% of American wealth holders.

As we have discussed, over this forty-year period, China has learned about business, capitalism, and competing on a global basis. They have adjusted their economic policies and contracting practices with American businesses so that Chinese companies and industries retain a larger and fairer share of the tremendous profits made from US and China trade. Good for China. What were they supposed to do—just allow America to exploit them for dirt cheap labor and contractual agreements that were lopsidedly structured in America's favor? Hell to the No! Over the past ten to twenty years, as China began leveling the playing field for itself, America has been crying foul play. Well, if America had spent more time fixing its own economy instead of selling it out to China, we would not have had to deal with this issue at all.

Former president Donald Trump's egregiously punitive trade policies with China increased the cost of goods imported from China by $80 billion per year beginning in 2018. This was massive but was just a precursor to the real driver of the massive inflation that America and the world have experienced since 2020. This trade policy significantly disrupted America's relationship with China. The world's two largest and most powerful economies, once synergistic partners, have now been transformed into rivals/enemies under Trump's hypocritical leadership. This strained relationship is one of the most important drivers of the dramatic rise in inflation over the past four years.

3. *Energy policies*

Drill, Baby, Drill: US exploitative oil and natural gas export policies have allowed America to export away all of America's economic comparative advantage for pure profits to the oil and natural gas industry at the expense of the American people and America's economic and energy security. Since the 1970s, every major economic calamity in America has been preceded by a run-up in energy prices because of the structural deficit in oil and natural gas supplies. However, with the fracking revolution in America and the tremendous growth in oil and natural gas production, America should never see a spike or sustained run-up in oil and natural gas prices for the foreseeable future. With the level of oil and natural gas production increases since 2010 from hydraulic fracking, gasoline prices today should be about $1.25/gallon, and food prices should be about 60%–75% cheaper than they are today.

Today, America is one of the world's largest oil and natural gas producers and exporters, with profits going directly and explicitly to the oil and gas industry's two million workers, who make up only about 0.6% of the US population. However, 100% of the American population uses oil and natural gas for fuel or feedstock uses. A true America-first policy would have retained a portion of US oil and natural gas exports (10%–20%) as a buffer in the American economy to keep oil and natural gas prices at levels able to restore America's cost comparative advantage relative to the rest of the world—in industry, business and for American consumers, while still allowing the oil and natural gas industry to flourish profitably and sustainably, and continuing to support the transition of decarbonization in our economy and society at a much lower price tag, because the price of fuel and everything else in America would be about half to 75% lower than what it currently is today.

Energy prices are the underlying source of all costs and associated inflation in the economy. Cost and inflation starts with energy, and then it seeps into every other cost element in the economy because the ultimate source of all costs in the economy starts with energy. This causes a cost-push metastasis throughout the supply and value chain of the economy that will not be controlled until energy costs are controlled, brought down, and sustained at economically competitive levels. America has the resources to achieve this end. However, the export policies pushed and sustained by the Trump administration in perfect step with the oil and natural gas industry have locked a structurally high level of cost and inflation into the US economy. It's not just Drill, Baby, Drill. It's also and most damagingly Export, Baby, Export. This doesn't seem like "America First" to me. Its export and profits first at the expense and catastrophic detriment to the US economy and the American people.

America's first priority should be to reserve strategic volumes of oil and natural gas exports for exclusive use in the US economy, creating the fundamentals for maintaining and sustaining the lowest business input costs on the planet in America, as well as establishing the fundamental basis for restoring the US economy's structural economic integrity and global leadership in the manufacturing and service industries. Being the world's largest *unconstrained* exporter of precious oil and natural gas supplies is pure profitability to the oil and gas industry at the expense of the wealth, health and security of the United States and the American people.

4. *Climate Change*

When former President Trump pulled America out of the Paris Climate Change Agreement in 2017, he put America four years behind in our race to save America and the world from permanent destruction and allowed China to move significantly ahead of the US in the development of technologies and industries leading and benefiting from the race to save our planet. President Biden has made significant strides to reestablish America as a leader and innovator in the climate change business and technology race, but it is hard to make up that ground after not just a four-year absence but also an administration that was aggressively holding back, resisting and destroying public and private efforts to achieve climate change goals and targets. Similar to when former president Trump pulled out of the Iran nuclear deal, the world is now much more uncertain about whether it can count on the US as a firm partner in the climate change challenge, given the setback that could raise its ugly head again if former president Trump is re-elected in November 2024. This potential uncertainty and chaos slows investment and growth in the decarbonization effort in the US and around the globe. This uncertainty and chaos is another significant contributor to inflationary pressures. Industries and companies will not freely invest with this level of chaos, not knowing what regulations and markets will align and support the development of aligned supply chains to make the cost and price of goods and services in the future as competitive, efficient, and productive as possible with the lowest cost to consumers and the business community.

5. *The Pandemic*

As we have discussed previously, probably the biggest source of increased inflation over the past four years is directly attributable to former president Trump's very deliberate mishandling of the Covid-19 pandemic for the purpose of dividing the American people to get himself re-elected in the November 2020 presidential election. The chaos he deliberately created is the primary driver of the excess inflation that remains in the US to this day.

Former president Trump demonized China, which prevented America and China from working hand in glove to contain the spread of the virus, principally in the provinces in China where the virus originated. Instead of letting his experts lead the discussions, Trump delayed by three to four months any serious action on Covid-19 and continued to communicate to the public that the threat was no worse than the common cold or flu while many died unnecessarily.

Trump's disbanding of the Global Health Security and Biodefense unit prevented the executive office from being prepared to lead the mitigation of the worst effects of Covid-19 when the outbreak first became apparent in October/November of 2019. US supply chains froze up and took years to return to normal because throughout most of 2020 the Trump administration continued to preach and enforce policy, saying it was not the government's job to get involved with the economy, that the free market would solve the Covid-19 issues on its own. All through 2020, supply chains were freezing up and prices were skyrocketing. This was a global pandemic, equivalent to a world war in terms of the number of people dying. These were anything but normal times. In periods of extreme chaos, war, global pandemics, governments must step in and act to keep supply chains from freezing up and using executive leadership and the full weight of the federal, state and local governments to make up for gaps that the market was not built to handle. Former president Trump is directly responsible for the worst effects of the rise and stickiness of inflation over the last 4 years because he failed to prepare for this moment by destroying the structures in his executive office that were created many years ago, to prepare him for emergencies just like Covid-19, and then when Covid-19 arrived, he failed to use leadership to blunt the freeze-up in the market by saying on many occasions, we are republicans, we do not believe in intervening on the market, because the market knows best how to adjust and protect the economy from once in 100 year global pandemics. Massive unaccounted for moral hazards is why thinking like this goes unchallenged and was allowed to infect and lead our economy during Covid-19, with the tragic consequences being spiking inflation over the last 4 years.

People demonstrated their support for Trump at the height of the pandemic by not wearing masks, not social distancing, and so on, while hospitals all over America were packed with Covid-19 cases, with patients needing treatment for cancer, hip replacements, etc. having their treatment delayed or canceled all across America. But in the face of this happening and people dying all across America, hospitals full everywhere, funeral businesses at record levels everywhere, Trump and his followers continued to say this was an illusion, this was a hoax, this was not real. The former president of the United States of America even went on national TV to tell American citizens that if they just injected bleach into their lungs, it would kill Covid-19.

A moral and effective US president like Barack Obama could have prevented the shutdown of the US economy and the need to spend a trillion dollars in emergency funds to jolt the US economy back to life. Injecting those trillion dollars into the economy by both former president Trump and President Biden did drive additional inflation, but it was not the cause of the inflation. The cause of the inflation was former president Trump, who caused there to be a need for the Treasury Department to print money to send to the American people to deal with the chaos created directly and explicitly by him.

6. *Tax cuts*

Former president Trump's tax cuts for the wealthy in 2017 have added $8 trillion in debt to the American economy. This money could have gone to fixing vital infrastructure for fighting against climate change, improving our educational system, fixing our roads, bridges, police force, health care, and so on. Former president Trump always talked about improving American infrastructure, improving health care, but it was all talk. What he did and demonstrated was using the power of the federal government to gain power and support for himself and to enact policies that made himself wealthier, like the 2017 tax cut, making the wealthy excessively more wealthy while leaving the rest of America with an $8 trillion debt ball and chain locked around the necks of the American people for many decades into the future. This is extremely inflationary because as the wealthy have become much more wealthy, they can spend wildly, causing the price of everything else in the economy to rise to unaffordable levels for the average person while the wealthy and well-connected are having a wonderful time.

This is not hating on the wealthy; this is the fact of how the economy has been operating to the huge advantage of the wealthy and at the expense and financial destruction of the bottom 80%. This is not bashing America. This is the fact of how our economy has been turned into an exploitative financial system, making the cost of living and doing business increasingly unaffordable with the passage of time, except for the top 10%. For them, everything is much more affordable because of the massive growth in wealth that they see in their portfolios year after year after year.

••

The Ultimate Con Game

The greatest challenge that America faces and therefore the greatest challenge that the world faces is that most Americans are no longer in love with being American, to themselves, to other Americans and to the rest of the world.

Being in love with America means you adore the idea of developing and becoming the best possible version of yourself. Being in love with America also means you are in love with working with other people in society and in the US economy to assure that others have the best opportunities to develop and become the best possible versions of themselves also. Finally, being in love with America means you are in love with working together with all Americans so that our communities, cities, states and entire country as a whole, integrated and working together, has the best opportunity and ability to be the best possible version of themselves—this, in principle, is the definition of a more perfect union.

When is a group of people the happiest and most successful? When everyone in the group has clearly defined roles that align directly with who they are and who they aspire to be, and each member of the group has the resources and opportunities to develop into the best version of themselves possible, and all the members of the group working together to be the best versions of themselves possible also allows the group as a whole to be the best that it can be as a team or a group.

This is a more perfect union because all the members love and want to be a part of the group because being a part of this group and working together, each member is actually able to be a better version of themselves, not just because of their own individual efforts, but because of the efforts of others they are working with and because of what they can do as a unified group.

Sports is an excellent example of this, and we also see this in orchestras, companies, etc.—all of the great teams, groups or organizations possess these characteristics. They are most successful, most happy and most motivated when they and other members of the group are working in the type of environment with the working conditions discussed above.

America is indeed a wonderful place to live and is still the best place to live on the planet, from a total societal perspective, right now. But the fundamentals that are holding America up are softening and deteriorating at a rapid pace, right before our wide open but blinded eyes.

Most Americans cannot see this because there are many Americans who are benefiting so excessively from the current system that they would prefer not to sound the alarm and would rather keep the party going, even though the medium- and long-term impacts on the US economy and American society will be catastrophic if we continue to support the status quo, or worse, go backward in our policy and market framework.

Because of the structural problems that we have discussed in the text so far, America's preeminence is not guaranteed in the future. America has only been in existence for 405 years. The other major countries of the world have been around for tens of thousands of years. America's arrogance and inability and lack of desire to learn from its history and from other countries' successes and failures has America on course to take an irreparable fall in the next five to ten years because of the problems we have identified in this text so far. And as I have said, I am not a negative doomsday preacher trying to scare everyone into listening to me and following my prescription for success.

Do I have a prescription for success? Yes, because I believe it is my responsibility as a citizen of the USA to proactively participate and lead where necessary to help preserve and improve on what has been the rise of one of the greatest nations that the human race has ever experienced on this planet.

Jesus Christ said, in principle, that the greatest leaders in the world are the greatest servants in the world. If you want to be great, discover what your best and most loved gifts, skills and talents are, develop them, master them, and then discover how you can become the best version of yourself by using your gifts and talents in the service of others in life.

Look at Amazon. Fifteen years ago, who would ever have dreamed that we would be able to go to our computers and order just about anything that you can think of, and that item could be delivered to you, free of charge, the same or the next day.

Which political party in America do you see talking about, promoting and establishing policies that bring all Americans together to understand and develop real, structural and sustainable solutions for all Americans and all the people of the world for the types of problems and issues that we have been talking about in this text?

What political parties or organizations are discussing these issues, getting feedback from the people about them and helping us to learn how we can work together to realistically address and solve these problems in our lifetimes or at a bare minimum in the lifetimes of our children and grandchildren?

I have not seen them. And that is the problem!

These issues and problems will not fix themselves.

Unfortunately, the problem is even worse than that. Not only are the problems not going to fix themselves, but we have influential actors in our society and our economy who are actually making the problems much worse with the passage of time, increasing the chances that America's best days will never return.

In reality, the time at which permanent economic and social collapse could come might be much sooner, with far fewer warnings or signposts because of America's deliberate and unflinching arrogance and narcissism.

So far we have only discussed the problems that need to be solved and our aspirations of what society could look like if we solved these problems (Chapter 1). But we have not proposed any real solutions yet. We will start to do that in the next chapter.

But the issue we are addressing now is the issue of leadership in American society and in the US economy. In my opinion, based on my observation, what the Democratic and Republican parties are presenting as solutions for America's diverse and complex problems are severely inadequate, and they are that way because we as the people are not holding these political parties accountable for:

1. Identifying what the real and relevant structural problems are in America that require solving

2. Providing real and structural solutions that actually work to solve these problems in ways where all Americans are involved in the solution and implementation process

This, in summary, is what the Republican and Democratic parties propose as solutions for America, in my opinion, which explains why America's economic and social situation continues to deteriorate for the bottom 80% of Americans from an economic and financial perspective:

THE REPUBLICAN PARTY: Keep taxes as low as possible. That is our money. We know best how to spend it. We don't need big brother taking our hard-earned income and wealth-creation money and deciding how to spend it. Secondarily, minimize or completely suspend government spending. Limit government intervention into American society or the US economy. Private business, private consumers and the market know best how to spend money and allocate capital in the marketplace. Government expenditures are a waste because government bureaucrats have no idea about what everyday Americans want and need to thrive and be successful in life, and because of this, central planning and expenditures is just a massive waste of money and the nation's resources.

THE DEMOCRATIC PARTY: Rightly criticizes the American economy and American society as being uneconomic and not working best for the bottom 80% of Americans while it's working excessively well for the wealthiest and best connected top 10%. Democrats' principal solution for making the economy more affordable for the bottom 80% is to borrow and spend money that goes to the bottom 80% to help them afford the artificially high cost in the US economy, driven by the broken uneconomical US economy, that itself must borrow and create uncompetitively high market prices in the US economy for the bottom 80%. Democrats understand structural economics and what is required to create an economy that works best for everyone, but I never see Democrats proposing solutions, working with Republicans, to address the underlying problems in the US economy that will be beneficial for all Americans, not just the bottom 80%. It's much easier to come up with programs that require increasing taxes and borrowing money to pay for the high cost of living for the bottom 80%, which eventually just makes the economy more expensive for everyone. Yes, it is helping the bottom 80% to afford the excessively high, unaffordable and uneconomic prices produced by the broken, uneconomic US economy, but at the end of the day, this approach is only making the problem catastrophically worse.

Remember, the goal of America is not unity—the goal of America is a more perfect union. Pandering by politicians to get us to agree, donate and pledge loyalty to their campaign and policy prescriptions for the sake of the unity of the party is not American. Remember, unity does not give a shit about whether you are becoming the best version of yourself possible as a result of supporting the party or the campaign. Unity doesn't give a shit about whether others are becoming the best version of themselves as a result of you and others supporting the party. And finally, unity doesn't give a shit about whether the party as a whole is working together to become the best version of itself because of our productive and synergistic working together as an integrated team.

The ultimate goal of unity is just to ensure that we are all at a minimum agreeing on the same thing and that we are 100% loyal to that same thing, whether that same thing is actually helping us to be the best version of ourselves individually and collectively as a whole. That is really authoritarianism disguised as democracy, and is probably why so many people have a strange sense of discomfort with supporting either party, because somehow they feel that their interests are not being represented the best that they could be.

Well, if you feel that way, maybe because what you are feeling is true!

But we can't sit back in judgement and point the finger and say, "See, I knew it. All politics is corrupt. No need to participate because neither party is adequately representing our interests."

The missing link is us!

Remember the famous words in the Preamble to the Constitution: "*We* the *People*, in order to form a more perfect union . . ." If our interests are not being represented, we must have the patience, persistence, care, creativity, empathy, and so on to work with others to make sure we are holding our public officials and business leaders accountable for doing what is best and what is right for all of the American people, both as a collective whole and as individuals in our states, cities, communities and homes. The solutions that I propose in the final two chapters of this book are meant to help significantly with this effort.

Which political party has a platform that comes closest to addressing the issues discussed in this text. I haven't seen it. I haven't seen it once in my lifetime, and in my opinion, this is the ultimate con on the American people.

And do you know who is most at fault? It's me, you, us, the voting public, because we allow our parties and candidates to dictate to us what is in our best interest without questioning it significantly enough to demand platforms, agendas and programs that actually incentivize and make our candidates give us a society and economy that we want and give us the best ability to be the best version of ourselves both individually and as a unified nation. The United States of America, not for unity's sake, but for a more perfect union for all Americans.

We are being conned to stay asleep, fight each other about issues and over problems that, if solved, would not make any significant difference in helping ourselves, others or our economy and society to be the best possible versions of themselves.

Sooooooooooooooooo . . .

Are you ready? Are you ready? ARE YOU READY?

IT'S SOLUTION TIME, BABY!

I am not God. I am not a world-renowned scholar or experienced politician or well-known principal from a prestigious US or global thinktank. I am Carlton Buford, a US citizen with an engineering and economics background who has worked in the US energy industry for the past thirty-plus years. My wife, Mary, and I have raised two of the best children on the planet, who are both adults now, and we have one grandchild, Niara Jasmine Williams, who is four years old and constantly tells her Pau Pau (me) to clearly know and understand that she is not Niara . . . but is rather . . . Princess Niara. Entitled? Yes! And I love every ounce of it!

These solutions come from my life experiences in all areas of my life—education, work, play, family, marriage, human and community service, etc. I'm doing my part to help make our society and our economy work best for everyone for both current and future generations of Americans and human beings on our planet.

Let's do this!

CHAPTER FIVE

Winning the Great Win-win: My Solution

I have taken time to talk about what the Economic Gospel for the USA is, what it looks like, and what the resulting benefits to the US economy, American society and the world would be if it is successfully implemented. The Misinterpretation of Eve is an allegory of the biblical creation story meant to set a new standard in the consideration of what constitutes moral behavior when considering macro-economic principles and policies related to the Economic Gospel for the USA.

Woke Alert: I propose that America's highest and most important value is not freedom but rather a more perfect union for all the people of the USA. The actual process of creating a more perfect union, economically and morally, creates both individual and collective freedoms that far exceed our wildest imaginations because the process of creating a more perfect union, economically and morally, is the handiwork of God, incarnate in the lived actions of humans working together in implementing and achieving this noble process with each other over time.

My goal in describing my solution, the Economic Gospel for the USA, will be on how the broken and uneconomic areas of the US economy can be repaired or improved upon, so that together these improvements and repairs will fix the US economy and make it fundamentally and structurally economic again, creating wealth, health and value added for all the people in the US economy, and not just primarily for the top 10%.

It is fortunate that we spent so much time discussing the problems in the US economy, because we'll use those problems as the basis and starting point for recommending which areas of the economy require the most repair or improvement and why repairing those areas will have the greatest impact on making the US economy economic and working best for all Americans in America and not just the wealthiest and most well-connected and powerful.

America wins the Great Win-win for America and the world by being American to each other and being American to the rest of the world. Ultimately, the mark of being an American is our commitment to create and sustain a "more perfect union" for all Americans. E Pluribus Unum. To save America and the world, America must lead the world by establishing relationships and commitments with itself and with the rest of the world based on E Pluribus Unum, globally.

What does that mean in simple yet complete terms?

Americans must lead by creating and maintaining relationships with itself and other countries the same way we love, care for, protect, develop and treat our own children. By putting in the smart, hard and creative work required to develop the masses rather than exploit them, creating the ultimate win-win, E Pluribus Unum. Let's discuss my vision for this in greater detail.

Vision

America's economy is economic, moral, true, just and fair, creating the strongest, healthiest, and most sustainable economic growth and value added possible—working best for everyone in the US economy, both now and in the future, driven by American's unique will and ability to love all other Americans as we love our own children. Remember the misinterpretation of Eve? God promoted Eve and rewarded her by giving her the highest gift and responsibility of all humankind—bearing and raising children to maturity. This gift is an act of pure love because it has no basis for naturally and automatically being economical and sustainable—this is the glue and secret sauce that makes creating and maintaining a more perfect union not just possible, but extremely desirable. The basis and drive of wanting a more perfect union should not be based on economics or meritocracy principles. The basis and drive of wanting a more perfect union should be the same basis that parents want to care for, protect and develop their own children . . . gratitude and love for the opportunity to grow and develop America exactly like we have gratitude and love for the opportunity to grow and develop our own children.

Dat's it. That is the secret sauce!

Mission: What must we do to make this vision come true?

We are our brother's keeper—it's our parent-like love for ourselves and for all other Americans, the same way that we love our own children, which commits all Americans to work, invest and play together in ways that proactively cause the economy and society to work best and grow the strongest by ensuring that all Americans *simultaneously* have the best opportunity *individually* to become the best possible versions of themselves, both now and for future generations.

Strategic Goal

Restructure the uneconomic, unsustainable and unaccountable US financial system into an economic, robust, resilient, sustainable, accountable and moral economy that works best for all Americans. This can be achieved by employing our allegiance to the highest and most valued principle in the US Constitution—we the people, in order to form a more perfect union—E Pluribus Unum—out of many, one!

The US economy is optimized and achieving its best results for everyone when it is built and sustained in a way where at the same time or simultaneously all of its people have the best opportunities, individually, to develop and become the best possible versions of themselves at the national, state, city, community and individual levels. A more perfect union! E Pluribus Unum—applied to the US economy!

This is absolutely not possible if Americans are not American to each other and the world. True Americans are in love with the challenge of winning the Great Win-win for all Americans, which is making the US economy work best for everyone, by working together constantly to create a more perfect union so that we all can reach and become the best possible versions of ourselves by treating ourselves and each other the same way we love, respect, treat, develop and graciously care for our own children.

Next, we're going to look at how we might implement my solution in a little more detail.

••

Strategic Implementation Steps: The Two Strategic Weapons of Light

1. Willfully Win a Quantum and Sustained Leap in US Economic Comparative Advantage

2. Willfully Win a Preamble-Focused Education Everywhere

Strategic Weapon of Light #1—The Big Picture

We can willfully win a sustainable quantum leap in US economic comparative advantage by creating the lowest business input cost to industry and manufacturing on the planet by:

1. Reducing American business input cost by $2–$5 trillion per year by using strategic amounts of US exports for much higher priority use in the US domestic economy, coupled with US consumer lead demand side management in strategic sectors of the US economy—together creating and maintaining the conditions for the lowest business input costs on the planet, repairing and making the US economy economic again, working best for all Americans.

   Another way to think about this is the American economy and the American people willfully putting themselves on a healthy nutrition and fitness program, where if we all work together strategically, productively and synergistically, our debt-infested and inflation-bloated uneconomic financial system can be transformed into a competitive, economic, sustainable and robust economy working best for all Americans in America.

   a. Willfully harness and divert strategic US exports (energy, agriculture, other) for fuel and feedstock for exclusive use in the domestic US economy, effectively shifting US commodity demand curves 40% to 60% to the left, creating conditions for the lowest business and industry input costs on the planet, causing primary US commodity prices to fall to these globally low levels on a sustainable basis going forward: Crude $16/bl, Natural Gas $1.3/MCF, Gasoline $0.70/gal, Wheat $2/unit, Corn $1.5/unit, etc.

b. Willful regional and national demand management by the federal government in partnership with strategic industries, business sectors and the American people, sharing the opportunity to proactively increase or decrease consumer/business demand for selected periods, regions, industries, sectors, etc. Selected and incentivized by the partnership between US consumers and businesses to minimize cost and inflation in the US economy, from a structural and economic market perspective:

For example:

i. To cut the price of meat and dairy products in half, strategically notified US consumers can willfully agree to reduce their consumption of certain dairy and meat products for say one or two days per week, or for two days per month, whatever is required for the people who are most capable and willing to support that effort that will achieve an economic price target that will make the economy work best for all Americans.

ii. To cut gasoline prices by 75%, American businesses and consumers agree to work from home and limit long trips for a specified number of days out of the week or the month—for businesses and consumers who willingly choose this option.

iii. Businesses, think tanks and government work together using economic research, machine learning/AI to automatically notify and recommend which segments of the population could most productively support these demand-side management efforts with the least impact on their lives while being compensated for their services.

Build out of the most productive and lowest cost supply chains on the planet for products and services Americans value most (housing, healthcare, education, food, transportation, energy, childcare, retirement), in US inner cities and rural communities, all across America, where economic development is of the highest priority. Unemployment falls to record but sustainably low levels as demand for workers in the US economy explodes with the buildout of the lowest and most productive supply chains on the planet, creating robust demand for reliable, high-quality and low-cost products and services both domestically in the US and globally around the world.

3. Willfully, economically and competitively increasing the supply of strategic products and services throughout the US economy by 5%–30%. The strategic products and services are the products and services that most Americans care most about: housing, healthcare, transportation, childcare, education, energy, insurance.

   a. Dramatic supply curve shift to the right for *strategic products and services* in the US economy gives new small businesses the capacity and incentive to grow business through competitive market share growth with superior products and services at price levels all consumers can afford without excessive borrowing or government subsidies.

a. Lowest cost product and service supply chains on the planet will support expansion of existing or buildout of new businesses, committed to providing consumers, products and services at a lower and affordable price for all consumers at high quality and reliability levels, restoring the brand and image that is backed up by performance and the reality that made in America is the highest quality and the best and most affordable price on the planet.

4. Achieving climate change compliance is a natural outcome of this proactive, willfully innovative national economic strategy step. This will not happen by itself: a miracle is required—our will to work together as a more perfect union is that miracle, embedded in the DNA of the Constitution of the United States of America! Let's get it, Baby!

••

Strategic Weapon of Light #1—The Specifics
Supply Side Intervention

Currently, the US exports commodities such as oil, oil products, agriculture and other strategic commodities. Strategic amounts of these commodities could be redirected exclusively for use in the domestic US economy as the first fundamental step to make the US economy organically economic and working best for all Americans.

As an example, the US currently exports 4 million barrels a day of crude oil to other countries, where that crude oil could be used in

America or placed in storage for use in America to bring the price of oil down to competitive economic price levels for the US economy.

Currently oil is priced at very uneconomic and monopolistic price levels, supporting uneconomic levels of inflation in the US economy. Over the past ten to fifteen years, if significant portions of US oil, oil products and natural gas exports had been used in the US economy to create and sustain competitive economic prices for energy in America to make the US economy work better for all Americans, oil and natural gas prices could have been and can still be today 50%–75% lower than current price levels.

The price of oil and natural gas are the most fundamental drivers or starting points to the cost of everything that works and moves in the US economy. Oil and natural gas are used as the fuel or feedstock for just about everything that we use in the US economy that matters and has any significance in terms of the cost that we pay for goods and services. So as the price of oil and natural gas goes up in the economy, the price of everything that oil and natural gas fuels or provides feedstock to also goes up.

1. Electricity

2. Heating

3. Gasoline for transportation

4. Food

5. Products and services, including:

    a. Homes

    b. Cars

    c. Appliances

    d. Furniture

    e.   Repair and maintenance of the above, etc.

6.   The cumulative effect of inflation in the economy starts with energy prices, which then impact all other costs in the economy, causing businesses to raise prices because the costs of their inputs are rising. This continues until it gets to the point that companies build these higher costs into their future expectations for doing business, with workers demanding higher wages and contracts to deal with rising prices from energy, the cost of food, cost of products and services in the economy.

This process feeds on itself for months, years and even decades as we have seen consumer buying power decrease by 90% (for the bottom 80%) from 1970 to today as a result of the fundamental destruction of the US economy.

All of this happened:

— because of America's economic imbalance in its energy supplies.

— because of the US economy's inability to grow its oil and natural gas supplies beginning in 1970.

— because of America's conscious decision not to prepare for the peak in oil and natural gas production that was forecast to happen back in the early 1950s, but the energy industry and politicians did not heed the warnings.

— because it was much easier to ignore those warnings and assume everything was going to be OK, like it had been for the previous thirty years.

Similarly, over the last fifteen years, when America had an opportunity to use the oil and natural gas fracking boom to rescue the US economy and make it economic again, those economy-saving supplies of oil and natural gas were just exported away to the rest of the world for profit at the expense and economic destruction of the US economy. For forty years, America was searching for an opportunity to create more oil and natural gas so that it would not be dependent on Russian and Middle Eastern oil supplies, and then when the opportunity was there, the exploitative profit motive won the day, as it has done throughout the most strategic points in American history.

Over the past fifteen years, the oil and natural gas industry has promoted and preached about the importance of energy independence and how producing and using oil and natural gas produced in America makes the US economy strong while at the same time exporting our spare oil and natural gas supplies to other countries, selling America's comparative advantage, its buffer against inflation and its opportunity to revive US supply chains and domestic employment.

America's huge comparative advantage in oil and natural gas prices could have created the lowest energy commodity prices on the planet, giving the US the lowest business input costs on the planet, setting the conditions to make the US economy economic and working best for all Americans both now and for future generations, able to better withstand the increased cost associated with the need to transition to a low-to-no-carbon economy.

This dramatic leftward shift in the demand curve for strategic commodities in the US economy can reduce strategic commodity price levels in the economy by a factor of 3 to 4 from current levels, providing the fundamental basis for reducing nationwide business input costs by $2 to $5 trillion per year when aggregated across the entire US economy value chain over time.

This fundamental strategic economic step, requiring leadership, approval and coordination from the three branches of the federal government and proactive support from affected US business interests, would create the organic foundation for almost immediately restoring America's economic comparative advantages in trade, creating the lowest priced, highest quality and most highly desired brands, with insatiable demand for American products and services both in America and around the globe.

This demand will create the fundamental basis for the reconstitution and buildout of the largest, most productive, and lowest cost supply chains on the planet with their associated sustained and explosive job growth, right here in the good old US of A, built-out in the inner cities and rural communities all across America, where economic and social development is needed the most.

Demand Side Intervention

An economy with a very low cost structure or the lowest cost structure does not guarantee that the economy will have low inflation or products and services with the lowest prices in the world.

A perfect example of this is the oil-producing countries in the Middle East, which have some of the lowest costs for producing oil on the planet, somewhere on the order of $10–$15/barrel. If it cost your business say $15/bl to make oil and you wanted to make a return similar to what you could get in the stock market for your business, that return might be 15% over the long term. So if the cost of making oil in the Middle East is $15/bl, then to get a return of 15%, the price of oil sold would need to be $15/bl × (1.15) = $17.25. Today the price of oil in the Middle East is about $85/bl, yielding a return of 467% annually on oil produced at a cost of only $15/bl.

Think of how much more productive and affordable both business and life would be if oil prices were priced at levels consistent with competitive economics that are moral, just and fair for everyone. Everything everywhere would be more affordable for everyone in the world. I bring this up again to make a point: just because a company or country has the ability to produce goods and services at a low and affordable price that would be beneficial for everyone, that does not mean every or any company, organization or country is going to do what is best for everyone if they have the power (ability) and will (choice) to freely decide what price to charge for their product or service, with little or no negative consequences. As we see with the case of the Middle East oil producers above, they will choose a price that reflects their profit motive, with little concern for how those prices negatively impact the rest of the world.

Similarly, in America, the price of housing, healthcare, education, energy, transportation, food, retirement, etc. has skyrocketed, increasing 5%–8% per year since the 1970s, while wealth and wage increases for the bottom 80% have been under 2% per year over the same period, perfectly explaining why consumer buying power is down 90%. Again, unless there are competitive economic forces in the US economy causing businesses to keep prices economically competitive and affordable for consumers, businesses will naturally use their market power to charge consumers prices significantly above what is healthy, just, robust and moral for the economy and everyone who participates in it.

Because of industry consolidation or structural problems of supply shortages in certain sectors of the US economy, the current levels of competition in the market are not sufficient on their own to incentivize producers to keep the prices affordable in the economy for housing, healthcare, education, energy, transportation, etc., primarily for consumers in the bottom 80% of the population in terms of wealth and income. Consumers in the top 10%–20% of the wealth scale in America are doing just fine with the prices of housing, food, education, childcare, with plenty of extra cash left over to fund retirement savings, etc. But that's for 30–60 million most wealthy Americans in America. For the rest of us, the other 270 million, life is not a beautiful walk in the park, and the opportunities for improving our conditions are limited and will become even worse with the passage of time, especially if the status quo of the last fifty years persists going forward.

What if there was a way to harness blockchain technology with AI/machine learning to alert consumers to how they could work together and bring down prices in the US economy to affordable, competitive, economic levels for the most important strategic products and services in the economy? Technology has and can continue to be harnessed to give significantly more advantage and market power to the wealthy and well connected to further tilt the US economy for the benefit of the top 10%, at significant expense to the bottom 80%.

That is what has happened to the bottom 80% over the past fifty years. We are in solution mode now. We are trying to restore balance, fairness and sustainability in the US economy and American society. AI/machine learning and blockchain technology needs to be aggressively harnessed and used to make the US economy work better and best for all Americans, not just those at the top.

Scientists and economists estimate that the power of AI/machine learning and blockchain technology has the potential to create the greatest advances in human history. The biggest question here is benefits for whom? Those who have the wealth, resources and power to harness those benefits and steer them to their own advantage are the same players who have been winning and maintaining an unfair advantage in the economy over the past fifty years.

Very deliberate and aggressive actions, laws and policies should be established both now and in the foreseeable future for harnessing the power of this technology to restore the balance of power in the US economy so that the economy works best for everyone and not just the advantaged 10 percent at the top. Not because of jealousy, envy, strife or vengeance, but because the lopsided nature of the US economy is driving it towards implosion, destroying America for both the rich and poor alike if nothing is done to change the current trajectory.

If Americans fall in love with being American again, to ourselves, to one another and to the rest of the world, AI and its associated technologies can be harnessed to have a miraculous impact on the US economy as well as the global economy as a whole. Responses to the Covid-19 pandemic in the US and around the globe demonstrated the power that collective and coordinated behavior changes could have on the economy and environment. The collective coordinated demand behavior changes driven by Covid-19 demonstrated that:

1. Energy and oil prices could be reduced by 70%.

2. CO_2 greenhouse gas emissions could be reduced by an all-time record amount, in 2020, down 4.6%.

3. Remote learning and work has much greater potential than previously expected.

4. Markets don't naturally adapt and change under sustained emergency conditions in ways that are most productive and sustainable for the economy or society.

5. Misinformation injected into traditional and social media can have negative ripple effects across society and the economy for many years/decades.

6. Conversely, well-coordinated, thoughtful, truthful information based on science communicated by trusted and vetted experts creates focused, productive, clear and well-understood actions which work and evoke confidence and trust from the public and the business community (e.g., the Ebola pandemic response).

What if there was a way to harness technology to help us to understand our individual and collective purchasing and consuming behaviors, both individually and collectively as groups of people, communities, cities, states and as a nation, to help us use this information under our individual control to make the US economy work best for all Americans? I can imagine when airplanes were first being used to transport people to different locations, there were many who probably said to themselves and tried to convince many others that airplane travel was unsafe and crazy: "If God wanted us to fly, he would have given us wings like birds. Why are we unnecessarily putting this added danger and risk to our lives by trying to fly when we're able to travel just fine on the ground? It just doesn't make any sense!"

We are at a similar point in history with AI/machine learning and blockchain technology. Harnessed the right way, this technology can more perfectly take advantage of helping Americans, individually and collectively, control the process of coordinating and leading the collective behavior choices of consumers in society or in our economy. This is not a process that we turn over to the government, big business or the computers themselves—consumers would lead this effort in partnership with business and government. *It takes a village!*

AI and blockchain-empowered digital currency could bring transparency and accountability to the marketplace for the individual consumer, making market prices transparently competitive and affordable based on the globally low cost of doing business in America. Collective, societal harnessing of AI to help the economy work better for consumers and businesses alike would work something like follows:

Regional and national demand management by the federal government in partnership with strategic industry/business sectors and the American people, sharing the opportunity to proactively increase or decrease consumer/business demand for selected periods, regions, industries, sectors, etc., further changing demand in the US economy, strategically reducing cost and adding greater fundamental and structural affordability to the US economy.

Examples:

1. Digital currency empowered by AI and blockchain technology uses government, market and our personal data embedded in our bank cards to instantaneously adjust the price that you pay for strategic products and services in the US economy so that they are affordable for you, based on your life situation. This would apply to products and services such as housing, education, healthcare, transportation and insurance.

2. Digital currency will send notices and alerts providing you incentives for deciding to purchase items later or purchase them earlier than you may have initially planned. Not pre-

venting you from making purchase at your desired time but providing attractive incentives for you to decide to choose to purchase at another time, sooner or later than you had originally planned.

3. Digital currency sends notices and options to you on how switching to specified products or brands helps make the economy lower cost, fairer, with lower inflation, better mitigation of climate change, and so on.

Again, it's one thing to make the economy structurally low cost with the ability to structurally create lower and more affordable prices for everyone in the economy. But just because costs are low doesn't mean businesses will automatically charge you a low economic price consistent with what it cost the business to make the product and service they are selling. It is human nature to try to sell products and services at the highest prices possible without getting into trouble with the government for price gouging or losing business from competitors because their prices are too high.

Again, this cannot happen if Americans are not in love with being American to themselves and to each other. It sounds corny, but it is actually the strong, smart, scientific, loving, faithful, patriotic, gracious and brave thing to do. The old way of thinking is we cannot trust anyone: we cannot trust business and we cannot trust the government; I mind my business, you mind yours, and maybe if we're lucky, we will all be OK and everything will work out.

For the top 10%–20% in America, this may be true. But for the other 270 million Americans, well, things are not working out so well for us. And the problem for all of us is that the US economy in its current state is not an economic and healthy US economy. It is really a Ponzi scheme headed for collapse in the next five to ten years if the status quo of the last fifty years persists.

I know that a lot of my solutions seem pretty big picture, pie in the sky, ideas that are nice to discuss and think about, but how does this come together to be useful for individuals, groups, and organizations who want to affect change in our society and politics? Most importantly, how in the hell do we get Americans to willfully fall in love with being American to themselves and to others? Good luck with that one, right?

In the final chapter of this book, I present a solution that I call "Our Solution," a specific solution based on all the principles that we have discussed in this book. Hold your butts, because we're just getting started!

••

The Results of Creating a US Economy with the Lowest Business Input Costs on the Planet

US trade and current account deficits will be eliminated, resulting from the restructured inputs to the economy, making it fundamentally much more healthy, financially solvent and economically sustainable. Redirection of strategic US exports for exclusive use in the US domestic economy will also naturally support the achievement of climate change net zero emission targets by 2050.

These actions do more than put America on a level playing field with low-cost Asian and emerging market economies; they actually put America at a significant economic comparative advantage relative to all other nations on the planet, opening the door for the US to lead and support the re-establishment of an economically healthy and sustainable globalization that is trusted, interconnected and not exploitative or protectionist but willing and able to trade with any country, anywhere on the planet.

If other countries can make products or services at a lower cost with superior quality to the US, we will buy them until we can beat the price and quality level, or we will just concede on that/those market(s) and focus on markets where we are better or the best and have a significant comparative advantage.

This is the first step in making America's economy both economic and moral. Here's how we will all benefit in detail:

Strategic Weapon of Light #1—The Benefits

1. Strong, healthy and sustainable economic fundamentals: interest rates 5%–10%, economic growth 3%–7%, inflation 1%–3%, job growth 3–8 million/yr, consumer consumption growth 3%–6%, saving rate 4%–6%, velocity of money 2–4, dollar index 140–170, unemployment rate 1%–3%, labor force participation ratio 70%–85%.

2. Lowest business input costs on the planet: $18/bl. crude oil price; $0.65/gal. gasoline; $1.0/mcf natural gas, $1.35/unit corn, $1.85/unit wheat, $3.5/unit soybean. Saving $2–$5 trillion per year or up to $30 trillion in US business input costs savings over the next ten years.

3. Quantum leap in US economic comparative advantages—winning business domestically/internationally with the highest quality at lowest prices, even with a strong US dollar.

4. Massive development, construction and reconstitution of US globally superior domestic supply chains and associated and

sustained domestic small businesses, meaning job creation—built-out in inner cities and rural communities in highest need of economic and social development, as the first priority, all across America.

5. Jobs and small business employment surges and remain sustainably higher with the build-out of the largest and economically competitive domestic supply chains on the planet, resulting from quantum leap in US economic comparative advantage deriving from the lowest business input costs on the planet, located in inner-city and rural communities in highest need of economic development—as the first priority.

6. High-quality and affordable housing, healthcare, education, transportation, childcare, insurance and retirement for all Americans—dramatic downward market price corrections eliminating the need for excessive private sector borrowing and government subsidies to pay for consumer consumption of these vital products and services—thus also eliminating excessive public and private sector future catastrophic debt liabilities related to healthcare, housing and retirement savings because these products/services are paid for affordably in the private sector when they are purchased.

7. Education, career, business, income and wealth equality of opportunity for all Americans—eliminating the school to neighborhood and neighborhood to prison pipeline in rural and inner-city communities across America. This is the big one. The reason we see thousands of crimes and murders every week, primarily in inner-city and rural communities all across America, is because of the lack of opportunities for

disadvantaged Americans to develop and grow in the communities and environments where they live.

8. Extreme partisan divide eliminated in America because now the fundamental drivers that create health, wealth and prosperity for all Americans require that all Americans work together as a unified team (a more perfect union) of people (a "family") to reap these benefits, both individually and collectively as a nation. We are willfully and lovingly obligated as a nation and as individual citizens in our nation to create and maintain our economy in such a way that our individual and collective economic interests remain aligned—to achieve and maintain this balance requires an explicit and continual act of patriotic will by all Americans.

This is the true definition of what it means to be an American citizen. When this happens, you will not see the stock market running up to record levels without bringing the real economy and all of the people in the economy with it. The goal here is to create an economy that specifically, scientifically, consciously and proactively creates and maintains provisions in our economy, such that every American has the best opportunity to develop and become the best possible version of themselves by making sure that everyone else in America has the best opportunity to become the best possible version of *themselves*. We're all in it together.

Notice here that I didn't say everyone should have an *equal* opportunity to be the best that they can be, but rather that everyone should have the *best* opportunity to be the best version of themselves possible. We are all different and unique individuals with different life circumstances and opportunities. What is needed to allow one person to become the best possible version of themselves may be completely different from what is needed for another person to become the best possible version of themselves.

9. Elimination of the need for excessive public and private sector borrowing to artificially support uneconomic activity, which would not take place without this artificial and uneconomic support. Support is no longer needed because the economy has been transformed to be organically economic, where economic activity is driven and demanded in the marketplace in a way that pays for itself, without requiring excessive financing, because the market activity is organic rather than artificial.

    Currently, many markets in the US economy are not economic or organically economic because the US economy has economic cancer, where many markets are broken and non-self-correcting. The Economic Gospel for the USA acts like a competitive economic market maker for the economy—creating and making economic liquidity throughout the economy so that key markets become organically economic again or for the first time.

    Economic liquidity is not cash or credit. It is changing the fundamental underlying conditions in the marketplace or the economy so that suppliers can profitably supply consumers with high-quality, highly desired products and services at price levels consumers can afford without the need for excessive private sector borrowing and/or government subsidies—*this is the moon shot; there is no higher priority on this planet than to win this mission and make it a reality!*

10. Climate change emission reduction target achieved as a natural outcome of the restructuring of strategic exports and

electrification of the US transportation industry, eliminating excessive current account and federal budget deficits and US public/private sector debt levels over the next fifteen years.

••

Strategic Weapon of Light #1—Program Requirements

$1.5–$3 trillion infrastructure build-more-than-paid-for program funded by low-cost economic savings in the economy—not yo' granddaddy's national infrastructure program. We the people, creating a no-free-lunch economy—competitive economic markets. The President leads this effort with support from the Departments of Energy, Transportation, Agriculture, Commerce, Housing and Urban Development, Health and Human Services, the Treasury, Federal Reserve, National Governor and Mayor's Associations, etc.

1. Redirect oil, gas, agriculture and other strategic exports for exclusive use in the US domestic economy, creating the conditions for the lowest business and consumer fuel, food and feedstock input costs on the planet, and thus creating a sustainable quantum leap in the economic comparative advantages of the USA. Harness the full diversity of the American people, business and industry to incentivize strategic and proactive (AI/blockchain ecosystem integrated with digital currency embedded with economy optimizing decision logic) demand increases/decreases for specified periods of time to achieve targeted strategic economic results. It is impossible to achieve by any other means, so quickly, so precisely and with such sustainably synergistic and quantum leaps in eco-

nomic productivity and price affordability for both consumers and businesses.

2. Build out and upgrade infrastructure in oil, gas, agriculture and other strategic export/import sectors, necessary to optimize a quantum leap in economic efficiency and productivity required to achieve redirecting of oil, gas, agricultural and other strategic exports for exclusive and much more productive economic use in the US domestic economy.

3. Transportation industry fuel switch: oil to electric, LNG exports to electricity generation, oil to biofuel, etc.: 80% of all forms of transportation powered by electricity by 2035. Balance of transportation services powered by renewable fuel sources or hydrocarbon fuel sources with carbon capture and storage technology that are 100% effective. National electric system powered by renewable energy or hydrocarbon sources with carbon capture and storage technology that is 100% effective by 2050.

4. Integrate smart cities with transportation system strategy and strategic national telecommuting program, across America, profitably, through market share competition that optimizes the lowest cost to the consumer and minimizes CO_2 emissions while maximizing convenience for both consumers and businesses. Total oil/natural gas demand reduction from commodity export redirection to domestic economy, fuel switching and telecommuting is on the order of 10–15 million barrels per day, oil equivalent, resulting in a 40%–75% leftward shift in the US oil and commodity demand curve in conjunction with upgrades to the US oil and commodity industry infrastructure. This will ultimately support indus-

try-wide profitable oil prices at \$15–\$20/bl on a structural and sustained basis going forward, creating a quantum leap in sustained business productivity, productive rebuild out of US domestic supply chains delivering the highest quality products and services on the planet at price levels consumers can easily afford without the need for excessive private sector borrowing or government subsidies.

5. Nationwide electric system build-out and upgrade to support rapid transportation fuel supply shift from oil to electricity. Electric system fuel supply diversification and fortification with—renewables, coal and natural gas with carbon capture and storage 100% effective, distributed generation/storage, demand side management, commercial/residential electric charging station build-out nationwide, electric transmission and distribution upgrade to support new demand for electricity from transportation, renewable integration, etc.

6. Build out commercialized clean fossil fuels carbon capture pipelines and underground storage technology.

7. Convert manufacturing sectors that use oil and gas for fuel or feedstock to use biofuels, electricity and/or deploy hydrocarbons as feedstock with 100% effective carbon capture and storage technologies.

8. Competitive economic market making in inner-city and rural communities in the highest need of economic and social development, as the first priority, all across America, for the purpose of building out the world's largest and most productive supply chains, in the form of small businesses, where applicable, and associated sustained surge in job creation, driven by the quantum leap in US economic compara-

tive advantage, resulting from the lowest business input cost on the planet.

9. Economically and competitively increase small business supply by 10%–30% in strategic sectors of the US economy, nationwide, in inner-city and rural communities with the highest need for economic and social development as the first priority. Strategic sectors include: housing, healthcare, transportation, education, childcare, insurance and retirement savings.

10. Building out nationwide AI/blockchain-empowered US digital currency ecosystem for each strategic sector/industry in the US economy (housing, healthcare, transportation, education, childcare, insurance and retirement savings)—creating and maintaining competitive market share competition for consumers at or below consumer affordability levels, for high-quality products and services in each strategic sector.

11. Use the lowest business input cost on the planet and consumer purchasing power standards in sector-wide AI/blockchain smart contracts to wring out high and uncompetitive "rent" in market prices for housing, healthcare, transportation, education, childcare, insurance and retirement savings

12. Market price correction as a function of income and other factors: For strategic products and services in the economy and for consumers in specified income classifications—sector-wide AI/blockchains serving these markets have price adjustment features in their smart contracts which modify product/service price level to the consumer as a function of consumer total household income, diversity population percentage, etc., which may be automatically applicable for a

given transaction. These competitive economic market-making forces remain in the market until markets can create this balance and matching in the marketplace organically.

••

Strategic Weapon of Light #2—The Big Picture

If you live in America and you have agreed to be a citizen, the Preamble to the Constitution tells us that our highest calling or purpose is to come together as a family of citizens for the purpose of creating a more perfect union, in other words, creating an economy and society that works best for all of us . . . because of and through the process of creating a more perfect union.

In order for an economy and our society to work best for everyone:

1. We must each willfully discover and understand what makes us the best possible version of ourselves.

2. We must willfully discover and understand what makes others the best possible versions of themselves.

3. Finally, we must willfully discover how working together collectively to be the best possible versions of ourselves as communities, cities, states, and a nation maximizes our ability to be the best possible versions of ourselves individually. This is what a more perfect union means. The way that we come together to work together to achieve individual and common goals makes our ability to achieve our individual goals much more effective and much more productive: the ultimate win-win for everyone.

However, similar to what we see and have seen in America's economy and society, America's education system is the best in the world for the top 10 to 20% of the population who can afford to have access to and experience those superior resources, but what about everyone else? And what does this mean for America?

Fifty years ago, American students were at or near the top in leading the world in all categories of ratings related to education: math, science, history, literature, research, new discoveries, etc. Today, American students no longer lead the world but are in the middle of the pack and declining steadily with the passage of time. Yet our most expensive and least inclusive (least inclusive by or because of cumulative broken unbalanced economics in America) school systems and colleges remain the absolute best in the world. Does this sound familiar?

The issue is raised not because of jealousy or hate of those who have the best educational resources in the world. The issue is that America is in decline and on the precipice of collapse because we are not doing what our vision, mission and strategy statement commands us to do, for our own benefit. We cannot continue to be content with just the favored few receiving the best education in the world. These opportunities need to be made available to all Americans for the betterment of all America. This is our creed, our belief. This is in our best interest. This is required by mankind to survive and thrive, both now and for future generations of Americans.

Remember our Michael Jordan analogy: the top 20% are smart and being trained to be the best of the best. But all of America would be much smarter and much better if the top 20% were being pushed and supported by competition from the bottom 80% also receiving superior educations, driving and creating excellence to levels beyond our current wildest imaginations.

Think of where America and the world would be now if America had made this a priority back in the 1950s or the 1970s or the 1980s or even as recently as following the global financial crisis.

If 1,000 pounds needs to be carried the length of a football field and an individual is asked to do that, most people would say that it's impossible. It can't be done. However, if fifty people were asked to do this same task, most people would say, OK, that's a reasonable request because fifty people divided by 1,000 pounds is 20 pounds per person. Most people can carry 20 pounds 100 yards without too much of a problem. But this assumes you can get everyone together, get them equally spaced apart and get them all to lift at the same time and all to go in the same direction together. If not, it will be just as difficult to get fifty people to move 1,000 pounds as it would be for one individual to move 1,000 pounds.

Leadership, unity and a more perfect union do not happen automatically by the invisible hands of economics. They happen by all Americans working together and treating themselves and each other the same way we treat, care for, protect, develop and encourage our children. This is the gold standard and the secret sauce to success. Remember, the misinterpretation of Eve taught us that children are an investment conditioned on unconditional love. Economically and competitively, having and rearing children makes no sense, but from a societal and US Preamble perspective, raising children and prioritizing our educational system is the greatest investment in human activity on this planet for current and future generations.

As the Covid-19 pandemic so precisely illustrated, the failure and never before seen horrific and unnecessary losses of life experienced in America were not a result of a lack of knowledge, resources, processes and procedures—the issue was our failure to love ourselves and each other enough to be who we say we are as spelled out in the Preamble to the Constitution. America as a nation has been in decline and Americans are losing because we are running away from our first love and increasingly falling in lust with the survival of the fittest, winner takes all, you're on your own, die and get out of our way philosophy adhered to by the top 10%, where the cards have been catastrophically stacked significantly and excessively in the favor of a small fraction in the economy since the formation of this nation nearly 400 years ago.

America truly is a great nation. But one of America's greatest and sustained sins as a nation is its lack of respect for and unwillingness to hold itself accountable for the reality of its history. Because of this, because it does not want to be held accountable, America keeps repeating the same mistakes. It ignores, revises or eliminates the truth and lessons of its history that would prevent it from continuing to give exploitative privileges and advantages to the most wealthy, well connected and powerful people and institutions who use that power to maintain exploitative control of the economy and society through continued lies and distortions about America's past, present and future, keeping the masses divided and viciously fighting against each other in direct opposition to the highest and most important value and priority of the Constitution—We the People, in Order to Form a More Perfect Union.

Not a better union, not a good union, not an OK union, but a more perfect union. That is America's highest value and goal; our union, our ability to work together, makes us so much better than if we work separately and apart from one another. We achieve so much more together, both as a collective and as individuals, because of the quantum leap in productivities achieved by the synergies created when harmonizing the rich diversity of talent and resources available in the population.

"Out of many, one"—This is a basic law of physics. If you have multiple and diverse forces available to you in an environment, if you can line the forces up to move in the same direction at the same time, you maximize the amount of work that you can get done within that environment.

It's much easier to just close our eyes and say, well if it ain't broke don't fix it; there's nothing wrong with our education system, students just need to work harder, get some discipline, get some religion, etc. The problem is, the system is broken for the bottom 80% and even for those school systems and colleges at the very elite levels in our country. They may be well resourced, but they are still missing the purpose of life, the purpose of America, the goal of America—a more perfect union.

If our education system is not teaching and preparing us to create a more perfect union, as evidenced by the decline in our collective education system, society and economy over time, then it demonstrates that significant reform is required at the highest levels of our education process.

Our education system must demonstrate what the Preamble means in words, actions, rewards and consequences so that our children have learned and lived experience of what it means to be an American and a patriotic citizen in America before or by the time they graduate from high school and so that they're proud of that, not because they have been brainwashed, but because they have found it to be true and believe it passionately from their robust, competitive, fun, rich, successful and rewarding thirteen years of educational experience.

Now I know many of you may be asking, "OK, fine, that sounds good, Mr. Ivory Tower, Mr. Elite, Mr. Economist. Now how do you take all that flowery discussion and make it into something that we and our kids can use, that is bold, beautiful, useable and helps them to apply the US Preamble in their everyday course and classwork from pre-K to graduation?"

Glad you asked!

••

Strategic Weapon of Light #2—The Specifics

We can willfully win a Preamble-focused education everywhere by:

1. K-12 *vision reimagined*: Empower students to discover their best selves and master their superpowers in the pursuit of careers or purposes which make the world a better place because of student contributions. This will create greater value added and greater opportunities for the student, the student's family and the community where the student lives.

2. K-12 *mission reimagined*: Student-personalized education AI process where each student has many options and opportunities to discover, try on, try out and master who they are, what their superpowers are and what career portfolio best suits them through a curriculum and daily lesson plan of activities structured into scripts, roles and role play—solving problems or capitalizing on opportunities in a fun yet competitively engaging entrepreneurial game framework, providing stu-

dents with thirteen years of real and/or simulated, work and business experience—ready to add value in the workplace or in higher educational pursuits before or immediately upon graduation from high school.

3. Industry-leading companies in information technology, computer gaming and entertainment will be harnessed to innovate tools, resources and processes that are standardized and copied while still being easily customized for differences across regions and within states and localities, but all drawing from the same template and principles that allow for exponential efficiencies and productivities in the education communication, learning, assessment and administration processes necessary to achieve the reimagined K-12 vision and mission discussed in points 1 and 2 above. Innovative and integrated processes make the K-12 public learning process orders of magnitude more engaging, competitive, inspiring, entertaining, and exciting than what students experience when they attend Disney or Six Flags parks, major sports events or concerts.

••

Strategic Weapon of Light #2—The Benefits

1. Opportunity: K-12 education equality of opportunity in America, *independent of zip code.*

2. Leadership: US primary and secondary students regain and maintain their top global ranking for education overall and regain and maintain the top ranking for all of the important education category rankings, *independent of zip code.*

3. Value: US students are college- and/or career-ready by or before the time they graduate from high school—in love with who they are, mastery of their superpowers and 100% accountable for where and how they will use their superpowers to make the world a better place while creating value added for themselves, their families, loved ones and the communities where they live, *independent of zip code.*

4. Experience: K-12 education process in America is reimagined and redesigned to simulate the entrepreneurial work place experience, in the classroom, serving as the means for engaging and creating thirteen years of real world work experience, skills (both hard and soft skills), knowledge and management relationship expertise absolutely essential for career or entrepreneurial readiness on or before students graduate from high school, *independent of zip code.* (The education process should be about preparing students for their careers from K through 12 as an integrally embedded part of their daily curriculum and lesson plan activities).

5. Passion: US K-12 Education engagement experiences are just as good or better than the engagement and sheer fun that students receive/experience when they attend Disney World, Six Flags and/or a major sports or musical entertainment venues by empowering students to discover who they are, how to master and show off their superpowers and where they can use them to make the world a better place while getting paid well for providing those services, *independent of zip code.*

6. Partnership: Parents, community, business and non-profits are bound and committed resources, not optional but mandated (we call this love) to provide students with abundant,

robust, diverse and comprehensive career/entrepreneurial *exposure activities,* helping students to be responsible for and accountable for <u>deciding</u> where they want to use their unique and connected superpowers to make the world a better place.

7. Economy: American economy stabilizes and grows much faster, stronger and healthier, with its economic benefits shared broadly across the entire US economy, driven primarily by a much better prepared and ready US workforce, made possible by the achievement of steps 1–5 above.

8. Life learning: Post-secondary school education and training programs for people of all ages, mimicking the program design of the K-12 education process described in steps 1–6 above, encouraging all Americans to invest in a lifetime of education reinforcement and growth.

9. Tuition: College education $2k/yr, online, any college in America: online college degrees offered at all major college and universities, with total tuition and fees for the year totaling no more than $2k, with comprehensive educational service offerings the same or better than services received from students physically attending the college or university.

••

Strategic Weapon of Light #2—Program Requirements

$800 billion–$1.5 trillion infrastructure build-out—Not yo' granddaddy's national infrastructure program. We the people, creating a no-free-lunch economy—competitive economic markets.

1. K-12 vision reimagined: see "The Specifics" point #1 above.

2. K-12 mission reimagined: see "The Specifics" point #2 above.

3. School curriculum and daily lesson plans re-imagined: Strategic sectors of the entertainment, information technology and computer gaming industries are incentivized and harnessed to support the creative design of fun, entertaining and breathtaking scripts, roles and script directing resources for K-12 curriculum and daily lesson plan activities that mimic or model the behaviors exhibited in successful entrepreneurial workplaces all across America.

Lesson plan activities and projects are the scripts and roles required to be acted out by students to achieve the workplace objectives for that day (same as lesson plan objectives for the day). The teacher is the director; the students are the actors. The behaviors required to be acted out by the students are the knowledge, skills and experience students learn in the context of real-world workplace scripts that are entertaining and therefore maximize the cementing of the learning process in the soul and spirit of the participating students.

During this process and over the course of the year, students get to try out different types of roles many times, so that over a student's thirteen years in school, they will learn, experience, be evaluated, master and fall in love with the roles, experiences, skills and soft management skillsets they have a passion for and are best at.

School now really becomes a celebrated and inspiring training ground and preparation center for student knowledge and talent that is marketable, motivated, ready, confident and qualified when students graduate from high school, no matter what neighborhood they come from.

Information technology and computer gaming companies work hand in hand with entertainment industry script creators to design the AI/blockchain-empowered information infrastructure, automation, social networks, CRMs and supporting communication resources/devices that allow teachers and students to focus on student entrepreneurial behavior, skill mastery and soft-management skills while the AI/blockchain-empowered and machine learning software and supporting tools and devices *automate* to the greatest extent possible the recording and capturing of student *superpower behaviors* for evaluation, assessment, remedial development-tutoring recommendations, student advancement and credential recommendations.

This process *seamlessly and automatically* measures and provides information on student performance, student performance diagnostics, student performance alert management (to students, teachers, parents and other stakeholders), student tutorial resource support option recommendations, student activity/project grading, student certification and student grade level advancement recommendations while supporting the individual student with an immutable blockchain transactional documented history.

The student's role and scripts are designed and customized to allow the student to maximize their ability to discover who they are, master their superpowers and discover where they want to use their superpowers to make the world a better place. This deliverable is the underlying truth and character-builder that demonstrates to individual students, their parents and coaches in no uncertain terms—truth that they can see and feel at the core of their spirit and soul—that they are fundamentally being educated from the inside out to maximize their potential so that when they graduate they are ready, able, marketable and in high demand from the world's businesses and organizations to help maximize the world's potential.

Educational product packages like Microsoft 360 with Microsoft Teams incorporates or has the potential to incorporate many of the features described above—using the exact same tools that entrepreneurs, professionals and businesspeople use to maximize their productivity in the business environment, giving students thirteen years of experience completing their business simulated projects and assignments with the same tools that professionals in the real world use every day, thus guaranteeing that students are really ready and qualified when they graduate.

Microsoft Teams/Zoom/Google will allow students to split up and work together in different groups both during class or during non-classroom hours, wherever students are, with the ability to efficiently share documents, data, etc. much more efficiently than if groups were physically meeting together without these tools.

Video conference meetings/classes also hold all students 100% accountable, because if they are goofing off or not paying attention, their behavior is being recorded. This solves meeting, group interaction and socialization limitations feared with remote learning. The primary issue with many remote learning ecosystems are that they are built as supplements to the in-room classroom experience. That framework misses out on all the opportunities that can be harnessed if the remote learning framework is not built to duplicate or mimic the in-person classroom experience but built to maximize the remote learning experiences that actually cannot be achieved in the classroom.

For example, look at the efficiencies and productivities that national and international companies achieve by harnessing video/telecommunications technology to run their businesses, allow their employees to communicate with each other and their customers and many different locations across the world. Businesses do not design their remote communication processes to mimic everyone being in the office together; they build them to leverage what the environment and activities which make doing work remotely more effective. Educational remote learning built with this vision/mission will take away the stigma and excuses about how and why remote learning is so ineffective and inferior to in-classroom education.

The education versions of products like Microsoft 360 with Microsoft Teams/Google would have to be significantly upgraded and customized to support the features discussed above so that use by teachers, students, administrators and parents is easy and intuitive, requiring little to no training. Like when you get a new phone: no instructions, but so intuitive you pretty much know what to do because everything is designed so that it works that way.

4. A personalized AI/machine learning process for each student is automatically incorporated into the education AI/blockchain ecosystem which documents each student's performance and uses this historical record of performance to help the student and their stakeholders make optimum decisions about the student's current assignments, projects and future education program choices, relative to student profile goals/

standards and/or relative to another student or specified groups of student profiles.

5. Education engagement process and experiences are designed to achieve/exceed the sheer fun levels experienced when students attend Disney World, Six Flags and/or major sports or musical entertainment events, independent of zip code. Activity and experience options and opportunities at school are so fun, self-revealing and engaging that students look at going to school like they look forward to going to a concert, sports event, a good movie or party/dance. The effect of this engagement level will have students demanding that their parents get them to school earlier and allow them to stay at school later because the learning and development process is so enriching and enjoyable.

6. Classrooms and school environments infrastructure are transformed into effective Hollywood studios: School building infrastructure, staff and staff organization are designed or re-designed so that classroom experience mimics as closely as possible the world of work, where students are passionately and joyfully discovering who they are, what their superpowers are and how they can use their superpowers in society to make the world a better place.

    School classrooms, spaces, facilities, resources, etc. should be designed/redesigned with the ability to quickly assemble the environment, props and structures necessary to perform the teacher's daily simulated workplace scripts (teacher's lesson plan activities) for the hundreds or thousands of possible different types of workplace environment/configurations that classes may want to act out in their class on a given day.

In addition to teachers who act as directors (instructors/ coaches), this teaching framework supports roles for teachers who serve as agents (advisors) and teachers who serve as mentors/caregivers (emotional/spiritual support).

7. Student electronic portfolio: Student Identity, Superpower and Career Development Electronic Portfolios (SISCDEP)— initialized in kindergarten and maintained through 12th grade, supporting student discovery, development and mastery of their unique and connected identity, superpowers and career aspirations—all documented in the education student/ employer supply chain contact network: AI/blockchain.

8. Student real-world training/exposure activity opportunities: A nationwide physical and/or virtual "warehouse" of identity-shaping and superpower-developing Student Career Exposure Activities (SCEA) providing students all across the nation, independent of zip code, the opportunity to try out many different types of potential careers or entrepreneurial activities, as much or as many times as they desire over the course of their K-12 educational experience. SCEA includes observation/imitation activities, projects, competitions, training, shadowing, internships, employment, and entrepreneurial opportunities physically in school or at hosted facilities, virtually via live internet, phone, virtual reality or video/ audio recordings. These Career Exposure Activity opportunities would be created, managed and sponsored by organizations, companies and government throughout America, at all levels—global, national, state, local, community.

9. Student/employer supply chain contact network: Students use social media-based student/employer supply chain con-

tact network to secure SCEA from companies or organizations seeking to provide students information, presentations, research, role modeling, mentoring, shadowing, training, summer jobs, part-time and full-time jobs—all for the purpose of providing students with career exposure activities to supplement their education with knowledge and experiences from the real world. These experiences are added to a student's portfolio of accomplishments that prepare them and make them ready and marketable for their next stage of life when graduating from high school. These Career Exposure Activities act as a recruiting and future employee supply chain resource for organizations and businesses that create these programs and experiences for students who will hopefully choose to work for the companies, organizations or industries after they graduate because they best matched their skills and interests.

SCEA experiences will be automatically captured in the student's SISCDEP over the course of their thirteen years in school, and this record will be used to help students make decisions on what direction they should take and what courses or career exposure activities they may want to pursue or repeat in the future.

10. Fun and competitive gamification of student performance: K-12 student individual education performance data can be used with permission of all necessary stakeholders to incentivize a fun, engaging, transparent and entertaining education and career motivation process where individual students, the teams they choose to be on, the schools they attend, the school districts, cities, states or regions of the country that they are a part of all receive scores daily based on individual student

performances. Participation by students does not require any additional activity or work. The performance data from their normal everyday schoolwork and extra-curricular activities are used to create their individual scores and the scores of the teams they decide to be on. Data from student performance is tallied over the course of weeks, months, quarters and the year, with recognition and awards provided to students during awards ceremonies for each of the periods of recognition (week, month, quarter, year).

The framework or model in which the game would be played is either an Olympics model (different teams from different locations) or an economic market model (different companies from different locations). For each period (weeks, month, quarter, year), individual students, teams within classes, whole classes, teams among classes, grade level teams, teams across grade levels, entire schools, teams of schools, neighborhoods, districts, cities, states, regions of the nation, and so on will receive recognition and rewards for the:

- Highest scores for that week, month, etc.

- Most improved scores

- Highest cumulative scores

- Highest cumulative improved scores . . . and so on.

The gamification can be extended further, into a type of fantasy education sports game where students and the teams that they are on can become "stars" in their local communities, across the city, state, region and nation, as the public plays the game, betting on students, student teams, and schools based on the different categories of performance for a given week, month, quarter or the whole year. This process can be used to help support and fund public schools while in a healthy, competitive and entrepreneurial way raise the individual and collective esteem and behavior of our students in a fun, entertaining way.

11. Private industry/sector restructuring and integration: entertainment, information technology, computer gaming industry, public/private US K-12, colleges, universities, trade schools, education and training institutions, education associations, parents, US profit and non-profit organizations work with federal government to restructure, upgrade, develop and/or create new industries/sectors required to optimize the achievement of steps 1–10. The President leads this effort with support from the Departments of Education, Labor, Commerce and National Governor and Mayor's Associations and the institutionalization of a competitive economic market making organization in the office of the President—incorporating economists, market strategists, and data scientists.

This concludes my overview of the direction America needs to take and what can be done to help Americans fall in love with being Americans to each other and the rest of the world, to save ourselves from ourselves and make this world much more wonderful place to live and thrive in for both current and future generations of all humans on our great planet.

CHAPTER SIX

Winning the Great Win-win: Our Solution

So, what do you think? Do you love my solution for winning the Great Win-win for all of humanity? Are you ready right now to put me on the ballot in all fifty states to get me elected as the next president of the United States of America?

If you do indeed feel that way or believe that, of course I am so appreciative that my message has reached you and we have common values and goals. But I am as sure as every breath that I take that there are many millions, maybe hundreds of millions of people who do not agree with what I have proposed so far and many who may be violently opposed to it. But that is a good thing. No one person, group or entity has all the answers for what would work best for most or all people as it relates to the topics that we have discussed in this book.

However, collectively, when we maximally consider each other's interests, needs and wants and are proactively working together to ensure that everyone has the maximum opportunity to grow and develop into the best possible version of themselves, we as a family of citizens on the planet are creating and maintaining the more perfect union, "Winning the Great Win-win," doing the Economic Gospel for the USA.

The Misinterpretation of Eve and the Two Weapons of Light strategies that I have presented in this text, in my eyes and from my perspective, are creative, bold, empathetic, moral, economic and strategically practical recommendations for saving the world from itself, for itself, in the next five to ten years. All the previous sections of this text describe why I believe this to be true from my perspective.

However, to be American in America, with the ability and will to win the Great Win-win in America and around the world, it is never enough to tell my story from my perspective alone. To truly win the Great Win-win for America and the world, I must have the leadership, creativity, empathy and truthfulness in my heart to tell my story through others' eyes and from others' perspectives—demonstrating my concern for the issues and priorities that others are challenged with in life.

Pain Points

Many of us—I would say most of us—have been and/or are hurting from something that we have experienced in life. Not just the poor, the victimized, the mentally unstable, but all of us, rich and poor, male and female, have had disappointments or very unpleasant experiences in life that have caused deep, painful and damaging wounds to our character, self-esteem and/or outlook on life and our view of people or certain types of people.

I call these the Broken Heart areas of our lives, where we have lost faith and trust in the belief that there can be any rational discussions about those topics, at least from our point of view or perspective on that particular issue. You may have been hurt badly or disappointed many times trying to understand and make sense of an issue or problem, where every time you have opened up and tried to trust or rationalize and make sense of things, you have been burned, humiliated, disgraced and made to look like a fool or even a monster, just for having your own opinion on something.

Personal Example

For most of my childhood, I would say from 2nd to 6th grade, I was excessively overweight. The kids in my neighborhood use to call me Fat Albert, or Tons of Fun, and would ask, "Why don't you wear a bra?" because my chest was so large and would hang down and jiggle when I walked or moved.

Over the years, my parents and I tried everything, but nothing seemed to work. I pretty much gave up and assumed that I would be Tons of Fun and the brother that needed a bra for the rest of my life. But then, in the spring of the 6th grade, every student at my elementary school had to get a health examination from a visiting nurse to record information that would be sent to the junior high school that we would be attending in the fall of that year.

I will never forget that day.

When it was my turn to go in and be examined by the nurse, she just stood there and looked at me. Her face had such a look of disgust, disappointment and disapproval. I had never met or seen this woman before in my entire life and then she proceeded to say these words to me. "My God, young man, you are about to go to junior high school! Don't you want to be able to run, play and participate in sports activities and have fun with the rest of your classmates? Don't you want to date and be attractive to girls?" And so on and on and on.

This was the most embarrassing moment in my life—this lady did not know me, but in my heart and in my spirit, what she was saying was one of the deepest and most painful concerns in my life, but I had actually been ignoring those concerns and putting them off to be dealt with at some time in the future.

The issue or should I say the opportunity for me was that the nurse showed me that "the future" was TODAY! That summer I lost 40 pounds in three months. When I started junior high, my friends did not know who I was. They said I looked so good and couldn't believe it was possible for someone to completely change who they were and what they looked like over the summer break.

Over the years, my parents and I had tried all kinds of diets, exercise programs, weight watchers, etc. Nothing had lasted or really worked. But when this nurse, who did not know me and who I had never seen me before, had the nerve and audacity to calmly but very directly and firmly pose questions to me about things that I was ignoring but were really the highest priorities in my life at that time, she woke me up. She made it clear that if I wanted these things I was going to have to be the one to take charge of myself and make it happen. No one else: you have to be in charge of you. You have to decide to do it . . . and do it!

Prior to this nurse talking to me like that, I had a broken heart when it came to my weight, my appearance and my hope and expectations for a normal teenage life. I was blinded by the failures of my past and was a prisoner and captive to those experiences and expectations of myself.

The nurse didn't provide me with information and facts about obesity and risks to health from being overweight. It was simply the way she looked at me, with pity and disgust that seemed strategically put out there to get my attention, to open my eyes to what she was really trying to do. She was trying to help me to see myself and ask myself if I really want to be the way I was for the rest of my life. She was telling me I had a choice, I did not have to be who I was then, I could be who I aspired to be, if I just took charge of being who I wanted to be.

At first, it pissed me the F*** off, like, who the hell does this lady think she's talking to this way? But by the time I left that office, for the first time in my life, I was in control of myself in relation to dealing with my weight problem. I didn't know exactly how I was going to do it, but I knew I was going to do it, and that is what I did.

The point I am trying to make here is that when we communicate with other people, many times it is not enough to just present facts, examples and our point of view on topics or issues to help people understand what we are communicating to them. To really get the message across, especially when the topic is controversial or highly sensitive, where others have views and opinions that are totally opposite to our own, it is vitally important that we step outside of ourselves and see, feel and experience what the other person sees, feels and experiences—take on their values, aspirations and goals in life and then package and bend your message to them in a way that helps them to relieve their pain, solves their problems and/or helps them to better be or become who they aspire to be, and at the same time use what you have said to them to most effectively open their spirit, willingness and attitude to best and most graciously understand and receive the message that you are communicating to them.

This will not just casually happen by itself, and it will not happen by you just casually giving it a thought and only halfway making an effort to see things from the other person's perspective with the attitude that "Well, I tried and if it doesn't work, it's out of my hands."

Hell to the no!

Like the nurse, you have to have the audacity to lead with creativity, empathy and truth that will heal the broken-hearted, bring sight to the blinded and set at liberty those who are captive, not from thinking that you are better and superior. You must communicate a story that engages with their point of view, their way of life and their life circumstances and elevates and respects them, making them see themselves better and opening the door for them to believe that they can and will aspire to be a better version of themselves.

This type of communication is one of the fundamental building blocks of democracy and the creation and maintenance of a more perfect union. Democracy absolutely starts and is sustained with how we communicate with each other.

The communication process that I described above is America—it is what it fundamentally means to be an American, the Economic Gospel for the USA. If Americans fall in love with communicating with each other the way I have described above and are actually in love with communicating with each other this way and to the rest of the world, the human family on this planet can truly create and sustain heaven on earth.

Again, others will not fully understand what we are trying to communicate to them until we frame our communications through their eyes, their concerns, and their priorities. It is impossible to credibly do this without making time to authentically listen, understand, research and value the other person's concerns, priorities and perspectives. It's one thing to speak to the other person's mind, logic and instincts; that is good and absolutely needed. But that is only half of the job. To really get the attention of the other person through communication, it is vital that you cut through the crusty barriers of indifference, ignorance, hate and fear and also touch and heal their spirits, their souls, their emotions, their aspirations for who they envision they are, to create and maintain trust in the exchange.

Even those of us who believe that we are level-headed and can equitably see both sides of an argument without being biased in reality are still using a lens that at its core is evaluating and comparing the differences based on our own experiences, knowledge, biases and beliefs. Real communication requires transmission and acceptance of messages between two or more people where the communication between the two sides results in a mutual understanding and agreement on the meaning of the messages sent by each party and a mutual understanding and agreement on any actions that need to occur between the two parties as a result of the communication.

In my experience, communication fails miserably when both sides are not assertively and consciously taking the initiative and leadership role upon themselves to proactively make sure that during the communication process with the other party, each party is committed to making sure that they are demonstrating respect, concern and care for the other party by making sure that the message that they are sending to the other party has been graciously shaped, packaged and prepared precisely and explicitly from the perspective, goals and interests of the party that is being communicated to. This lets the party that you are communicating with understand that you recognize who they are and who they believe you should know they are.

OK, so before we discuss my proposed solution for helping America and Americans be better Americans by communicating more effectively with one another, especially under the circumstances when the two communicating parties have totally opposite views, values and aspirations about life and are dramatically opposite on the specific issue or topic that is up for debate or discussion, let's examine the nature of the concept and the reality that opposites fundamentally are attracted to each other.

This is true in nature, in life and even in inanimate objects in the universe. We will look at what implications and conclusions can be drawn from this analysis for effective communications between people who think and believe totally opposite things to one another.

OPPOSITES ATTRACT

Opposites attract! This is quite easy to see in a direct sense when we consider the electric forces pulling an object with a positive electric charge closer and closer to an object with a negative electric charge. Or when we consider the magnetic forces pulling an object with a north magnetic pole closer and closer to an object with a south magnetic pole.

However, as a general principle, whether objects are living creatures or non-living objects, everything in the universe is made of energy. As a general principle in the universe, energy is always seeking to move from its current energy state to a lower, more stable and more efficient energy state. Moving from a higher, less stable, less efficient energy state to a lower, more efficient, more stable energy state is the same principle as "opposites attract."

The higher, less efficient and more unstable energy state is the opposite of the lower, more efficient, more stable energy state. Objects (live or inanimate) at a higher, less efficient, and less stable energy state or energy level are always attracted to or are always seeking to get to a lower, more efficient, and more stable energy state by the immutable laws and forces that have existed in the universe forever. Some people call this the "hand of God."

This general principle of energy (which all objects in the universe are made of, living or non-living) naturally seeking a lower, more efficient, more productive, and more stable energy state is in perfect alignment with the notion of E Pluribus Unum and democracy: We the People, to form a "More Perfect Union." Our differences should naturally attract us to one another. Our differences create opportunities for us to see, think about, and create new ways to solve problems that we could have never seen before had we not come together to learn from each other and harness each other's talents.

By coming together to mutually capitalize on our differences, we are just naturally fulfilling the natural laws of the universe—opposites attract for the purpose of moving to a more stable, more efficient, more productive energy state which in scientific terms is moving to a lower energy state. Less energy is required in the lower energy state, because in the lower energy state, we have figured out how to live, work, learn and play together more efficiently and effectively, because we capitalized on our differences to make that happen.

OK, I will accept the Nobel Prize for Chemistry, Quantum Physics, Sociology, Economics and Peace (Move over, Martin!) . . . Thank you (*bow*) . . . Thank you (*bow*) . . . Thank you (*bow*)! (Please excuse my delusional ego, but I am also a flawed human being ☺)

So if all energy is naturally attracted to opposites so that the opposites can transact and together move to a lower, more efficient, more productive and stable energy state, better and best for all, why are we not seeing people in America and all over the world, who are so polarized and so hating on one another, just "naturally" coming together, seeing their differences as opportunities to work together, to create solutions that will satisfy both sides at levels that would exceed their wildest expectations? (Yeah, Mr. Want-Ta-Be-A-Nobel-Prize-Recipient, WHAT ABOUT THAT? LOL.)

OK! Glad you asked!

The answer is indirectly implied in the question itself: "Just 'naturally' coming together . . ."

In the universe there is another immutable or universal law that all objects are subject to or obey in terms of how objects move, respond, react or behave in the reality of space and time. If an object is at rest or still, it will remain at rest or still until another energy force pushes or moves it. So we need to modify our definition above about objects always wanting to move to a lower, more efficient and more stable energy state. A more complete statement would be that "when an object is pushed or moved by another energy force, that object will seek its opposite, meaning it will seek or be attracted to move to a lower, more stable, more efficient energy state."

Another way to state this is that if an object is in a higher energy state, that object will not and cannot move to the lower, more efficient and more stable energy state if there is not a "first mover energy source" that proactively and purposely pushes or moves the object so that it can seek, move or be attracted to the lower, more efficient and more stable energy state.

Imagine a massive, 50,000-pound boulder sitting near the edge of a cliff that is 5,000 feet above ground. The cliff that the boulder is sitting on is narrow, but just wide enough to prevent the boulder from rolling off the cliff and smashing down to the ground below. The boulder has been sitting there for the past 500 years. The boulder's lower, more efficient and more stable energy state would be for the boulder to be on the flat and wide ground, 5,000 feet below the cliff. But the boulder has been on the cliff for 500 years and will likely stay on the edge of the cliff for another 500 years, unless there is some energy force that pushes or moves the boulder so that the boulder can be attracted to its lowest and more efficient and stable energy state, 5,000 feet below the cliff.

This helpfully explains precisely why people with intensely polarizing and opposite views on major issues are not automatically attracted to each other by the immutable laws of energy to find a better solution for both sides.

Inanimate objects like the 50,000-pound boulder will not move to a lower, more stable energy state until there is a catalyst or first mover energy source that moves the object from its still or motionless position to another position or location. We know from observation and the laws of the universe that when the object is put in motion, it will find its way to a lower, more efficient and more stable energy state, opposite to its current and higher energy state.

Analogously, for people who are diametrically opposed to each other on an issue or topic, they will not automatically be attracted to each other for the purpose of creating and winning a better win-win solution for both groups, unless both communicators become _catalysts_, proactively and constantly learning and discovering new ways to harness and use the other communicator's differences as resources for proactively creating a better or the best win-win solution for both sides.

Let's step back for a moment so we can more fully understand what has been said here in terms of what it means to be a catalyst, a first mover and the ability to unlock the powers of opposite attracting forces that automatically move us to a lower, more efficient and more stable energy state, creating the best win-win for all.

How was the universe formed? How did everything get here? The greatest minds tell us that billions and billions of years ago, there was a big explosion that caused the universe to be formed, and ever since that explosion, all particles or matter which are made of energy have been moving and combining with other particles or matter, all moving to their lowest energy state, being pushed by that first massive explosion in the universe to eventually form everything that exists today. But what the scientists and greatest minds have not been able to explain is what caused the first explosion.

Actually, they have answered the question, but they just don't know it. We know from science, observed facts and from our everyday lives that an object that is at rest or still is going to stay that way until something outside of itself moves or pushes it. So if the universe did not exist at some point in the past or if it existed but was not in its current form, something outside of itself had to move or push it, to get it starting to form and make everything that exists today. Something outside of itself, bigger and stronger than the universe itself, what could have been the "first mover" to move or push the universe hard enough to get it forming everything by moving to its lowest and most efficient energy state: God!

Man is the first and only creation on the planet, as far as we are aware, with the ability to be totally self-aware, the ability to learn how to learn and use that information to change our environment and fundamentally change how we live and exist in the world, based on the choices that we make from what we have learned, created and implemented in our environment since the beginning of man's existence on this planet. All other objects and animal forms on this planet are captive to living according to their instincts and the limitations that the environment places on them. It took birds billions of years to evolve and adapt to become a species that grew to a certain body size, shape, and weight and developed wings so that it could fly.

Over the course of about fifty to one hundred years, man/woman taught themselves how to fly, not by evolving over billions of years so that we grew wings, but by learning to become a creator, like God, the first mover, pushing, moving, manipulating things outside of ourselves. Through self-evaluation, self-reflection and consciousness, we have learned how to learn, for the purposes of creating things outside of ourselves, changing things and our environment to make life better and easier for everyone.

In the Bible, it says that of all the creatures that were formed in the universe, only man/woman were made in the image and likeness of God with the ability to be and act like God, with the ability to create for the purpose of making life richer and better for everyone . . . *by our choice*! This is the unique feature of God and man who was created in the image and likeness of God: we have a choice. We can decide to create or not to create. And if we decide to create, we can decide to create to make life better for all or we can decide to create to make life better for some or worst of all we can decide to create and make life worse for everyone.

This is why the Economic Gospel for the USA says that we have to proactively and willfully win the Great Win-win in life. It is not going to just naturally fall in place, unless we choose to go after it and make it happen. The universe is set up so that if we want to make life better for everyone, the universe is actually structured to make that happen, as long as man/woman *chooses* to follow that path.

That is good news. But if man/woman make choices that work against the natural structures that have been set up in the universe, energy will be less efficiently and less productively utilized, causing destructive, life-sapping entropic heat and heat energy which is dispersive, chaotic, creating separation and polarization—causing us to polarize and repel from and against each other, rather than attracting to and working closer and more efficiently and productively together.

Now let's bring this back to communications and willfully and proactively winning the Great Win-win. The Economic Gospel for the USA is really all about how we communicate. Democracy is impossible without this and explains precisely why in many areas of American society, it seems like democracy is on her deathbed and many are ready to bury her and bid her a fond farewell!

As human beings, we have the ability to choose to be empathetic, go outside of ourselves, and see ourselves as others. Like God, we have to use our self-awareness, creativity and love for ourselves and for others to communicate to them that we feel their pain, their sorrow along with their joy, aspirations and hopes for the future and we freely and lovingly demonstrate we care for and respect what they are going through and where they are trying to go. We can then follow that communication with a win-win recommendation that demonstrates that we can both achieve what we want and where we are trying to go much better by working together rather than just working on our own or, worse yet, working against each other.

Conversely, we as humans also have the ability to choose to ignore what other people are thinking and feeling or worse, hatefully use that information to make the other person believe that you are a friend who wants to work with them to create a win-win, and you gain their trust by creating a win-win that is really a lie; in reality it is a win for you and a big loss for them, but you don't care as long as you win without being negatively affected and whatever happens to them is just too bad.

That is an example of exploitative, moral hazard behavior which destroys relationships with people and if it happens continually with a large and growing number of people, it causes polarization, mistrust, despair and loss of faith. It seems like America, as well as the world, is becoming more broken, disconnected, polarized, untrusting, with less and less ability or desire to love and trust each other for the purpose of working together to make life better for everyone.

It feels and seems like the reality and truth about life is that life is really about selfishness, power, dog-eat-dog. Get what you can while you can and forget about everyone else because no one is coming to save you when you fail or fall on your face. Legal or illegal, as long as you don't get caught, that's the reality of life, the quicker you learn this and start behaving like this, the better off you will be in life. But this is exactly why America and the world economy and societies are on the verge of imploding, right before our eyes.

The universe and the laws which govern the energy and everything that exists in the universe were made/designed so that if we worked together to make the best choices for how we learn, play and work together, human civilization and the environment in which we operate would be more perfect, operating in its most efficient, productive, stable, lowest energy state possible, inhabiting, re-creating, and developing new resources for optimal living conditions on this planet.

However, because humankind has not sought to optimally work together and in many cases has decided to work aggressively against each other, the earth is increasingly creating chaos, confusion, separation, polarization, friction and heat, operating at a much higher, much more inefficient and much more unproductive and unstable energy state. The earth is and has been warming at a destructive and soon to be irreversible rate since the US and the world decided to financialize the US and global economy back in the early 1980s following the Great Inflation of the 1970s.

At that time there was an opportunity to learn from the mistakes of the past, learn from each other and fix our broken economy, but the US and the world took the easier and much quicker path of least resistance, and instead of fundamentally restructuring our economy and making it work best for everyone, we decided to financialize the economy, growing it uneconomically and dealing with the catastrophic losses that the financial system has been creating every year over the last forty to fifty years, until it breaks permanently—and it will, it's not if, it's when, *if we do nothing and stay on the current course.* Global warming and its planet-destroying outcome is another crisis created by humankind's behavior and decision to live selfishly and undemocratically together.

OK, Mr. Wanna-Be-A-Nobel-Prize-Winner, what's your solution or, as the title of this section of your book suggests, what's our solution?

To create communication that allows both sides to benefit from the Great Win-win, both parties have to be responsible and exert leadership, creativity, empathy and truthfulness to themselves and the other party. This will take time and effort, not an unreasonable amount of time and effort, just enough to consider the reality that the person we are communicating with is both different from us and just like us. Their differences are an opportunity to help us achieve or acquire something that we could not have possibly achieved on our own and without them, while our commonality or sameness gives us the ability and patience to see, understand and feel that we are the same in so many ways and because of that, we can see why we should make time to treat them the same way we would like to be treated by others.

Making love is wonderful when you are fulfilled in the process of making love. But making love reaches and exceeds its highest expectation when both partners are proactively working to win and making sure that the other person is being maximally fulfilled at the same time that they are being maximally fulfilled. Love-making, yes, think of it like that. A good way to think about the communication process that is democratic and creates the best win-win possible for both parties is as a communication process that is very similar or identical to love-making. True democracy, more perfect union, is communication among Americans who are in love with being American and who should want to fall in love with communicating with each other in a democratic way because this type of communication is just like making good love to each other. Do I get your vote for the Nobel Prize yet? ☺☺☺

"NO and HELL to the NO!" "You've given us nice little scientific and flowery examples of what it means or what it might be like to communicate with each other in ways where we can maximally work together with each other on this planet, but we need real solutions. What do you have for that?"

Again, glad you asked that. I'm creating a service that incentivizes very polarized groups to use the same differences that cause them to hate or even want to kill each other as the fuel and feedstock that will pull them together to create mutual solutions that far exceed each group's wildest expectations. I call this service…

ICU (I See You)—More Perfect Union debates

In the previous section of this text, I presented *my* version/vision of the truth and what I believe the US and the world needs to do to save itself from itself and create a just, moral and economic economy and society in the US and throughout the world. But that is *my* view and my perspective. ICU debates provide a very unique way to "summon God" to the debate process and allow *we the people* to proactively and graciously value each other's differences and similarities to create solutions that exceed debate participants' wildest expectations. Doing the Economic Gospel for the USA is really just doing the US Constitution, creating and maintaining the conditions for a more perfect union for the people and by all the people.

In the US and around the world, political leaders are shaping and framing the messages that will determine the quality of our lives or even our very existence over the next three to five years for both current and future generations. In so many instances, the messages, conversations and debates that we currently have do nothing to enlighten the public or give us a solid basis for decision-making. In many cases, the discussion and arguments don't even evaluate information that helps the public understand the most important issues or how effective the candidate will be in ensuring that he or she has the leadership capabilities to deliver on the proposals being recommended.

In many cases, the discussion is focused on a candidate's personality, constituents' cultural biases and the blame game, which turns conversation or debate into a reality show where both sides dig into their trenches and see which candidate is best at embarrassing and tearing down the character and personality of the other.

I believe this perfectly explains why the polarization levels have returned to such historic highs in the US and around the world today: exploitative leadership that uses its power to divide the masses and prevents them from holding leaders accountable for their actions, causing more poor unaccountable actions, policies and market failures adversely impacting the bottom 80% of the population so that the top 10% retains and catastrophically increases its wealth, power and control over society and the economy.

Another important component of this mass exploitation and manipulation game is the apathetic behavior of the masses—the masses not taking it upon themselves to make the time and expend the effort to hold candidates accountable and responsible for their conversation, language, recommendations, promises and policies. We get the political and business leaders that we vote for and that we pay for in terms of buying their policies, products and services. We the masses must make the time and effort to do a much better job at holding our leaders (both political and business leaders) to account so that they are motivated to really represent our individual and collective best interests.

No wonder our leaders and leadership do not feel accountable or responsible to the public, because the processes that we use to hold them accountable for what is in the public's best interest do not exist. The discussions and issues that we have with our leaders are superficial and rarely deals with the real problems and pain points in society that need to be identified and communicated to with the public so that the communication process feels like and is like making good love. Where is that happening?

ICU (I See You) More Perfect Union debates are specifically for the purpose of holding everyone more accountable (leaders and the masses whose interests the leaders are supposed to be representing) in actually dealing with the issues under consideration in the debate and creating solutions that both sides can best agree to as most effectively dealing with the issues under consideration.

Let's review in more detail now what these ICU debates are and how they can be used to win the Great Win-win for America and the world:

ICU—What is it?

I have a novel idea: how about a debate process that by its very nature incentivizes and keeps leaders focused on identifying the real and underlying problems causing the issues under discussion in our national debates? I have another novel idea: once the problems have been identified that are actually causing the issues being debated, how about focusing on those problems specifically to actually come up with solutions that exceed the wildest expectations of both sides of the debate?

Finally, what if the audience in the debates were allowed to explicitly be involved in the debate, evaluating and judging debaters' arguments and judging them for their demonstrated behaviors of leadership, creativity, empathy and truthfulness dynamically in real time? And what if we rewarded the audience for their judging and evaluation services by giving them the opportunity to also be winners in the debate, based on the points they accumulate, demonstrating their truthfulness and fairness in evaluating debaters in real time, with audience truthfulness scores sorted in rank order, displayed in real time, with the public able to see which audience participants are leading the debate in terms of their truthfulness and fairness in evaluating debaters? This gives the audience, who are acting as judges, an incentive to evaluate the ideas, behaviors and arguments of the debaters as fairly and carefully as possible.

For any given debate, the audience's cumulative scores for the debaters will determine who wins the debate, and the audience or judges' truthfulness and fairness scores will determine which audience members will also be winners in the debate.

This gamification—the scoring, awards and the assignment of winning and winners of the debate—will make the debate process much more engaging, competitive and fun, but the real value in this is what will be learned from the debate process itself. Participation in or just watching this debate process will be a potentially life-changing experience in and of itself. The issues discussed, the pain points wrestled with and the solutions created from the depths of pain and redemptive confessions shared between debaters will be of the likes which have not been seen or experienced in an open public forum before, on the critical issues in life, from opinion leaders that the public care about and value the most.

Debates will be produced, marketed and promoted like prize fights, but in this competition, the focus of attention will not only be on the debaters in the ring, but also on the audience participants who are also there competing with each other and the debaters to create an arena where the consciousness of reality is summoned who fills and saturates the atmosphere with an unquenchable but gracious passion for creating and maintaining a "more perfect union" among all the participants and observers of the ICU (I See You) More Perfect Union debate experience.

EXAMPLE (a fictional scenario for demonstration purposes)

Biden vs. Trump debate

ICU debate topic: Making the US economy work best for all Americans

It's a warm early fall evening, Wednesday, September 18, 2024, coming up on 7:00 p.m. in Dallas, TX, at the multibillion-dollar Dallas Cowboys multipurpose football stadium, the scene of the first presidential debate between President Joe Biden and former president Donald Trump, on the topic of inflation and the economy.

Trump was nominated by the Republican Party as their candidate back in March of this year, with former South Carolina Governor Nikki Haley giving former president Trump a respectable challenge but eventually losing to him, getting a sizeable number of votes in the final runoff.

Just two months ago, former president Trump was convicted on all charges against him related to the January 6, 2021, insurrection. The former president has appealed the ruling, which is now before the Supreme Court, with a new ruling not expected until December of this year, well after the 2024 US presidential election.

Former president Trump is currently out of jail on a bond of $50 million, and like in the past, uses his legal jeopardy as a tool to paint himself as a victim of the corrupt Biden administration, which has created these charges out of thin air to prevent the former president from having an opportunity to run for president again and win.

Many of the public believe Trump's lies about being a victim and that the current president is using the power of the federal government to create false charges against him, causing the former president's poll numbers to rise every time he is charged or convicted of a crime.

Prior to Trump's July 2024 conviction, Biden and Trump were neck and neck at the polls, with Biden having a slight 2 percentage point lead. Since Trump's conviction in July, he has been consistently leading in the polls by a whopping 15 percentage points, well above any possible error in the polling, and appears to be headed for an easy retaking of the White House, given the heavily promoted view that the former president is the victim of a powerful and corrupt US justice system that is unfairly persecuting him.

President Biden and former president Trump both agreed that their first debate would be an ICU debate. ICU debates were first introduced onto college campuses in July 2024 and went viral immediately on social media across America and around the world. In less than three months, ICU debates have become the gold standard for truth discovery, problem resolution and redemptive more perfect unity creation and maintenance between extremely polarized groups.

Trump and his team were initially opposed to the ICU debate format, but following his conviction on all charges associated with the January 6 insurrection case, part of the condition of his being released from jail on bond and to being allowed to continue campaigning required that all three of his presidential debates be of the ICU debate format. Public opinion and the polls also demanded this, giving the former president an opportunity to clear himself in the court of public opinion with a debate process that is widely and highly respected by people on the far right, the far left and those smack dab in the middle.

Ticket sales for this event are right at 104,500 people. The seating capacity for the Dallas Cowboys stadium is 80,000 with a total attendance capacity of 105,000 if standing room is allowed. The average ticket price is about $5,000 per person, with 20,000 seats reserved for *between $20 and $100 to allow everyday working people to experience this event in person.*

Celebrities, entertainers, athletes, opinion and world leaders across America and around the world are in attendance and will be serving as judges in this debate. Audience fairness and truthfulness scores will be posted in real time during the debate in rank order, showing in real time which audience participants are leading in the competition to provide the most truthful and fair judging of the presidential candidates' responses.

The general public not participating as judges in the debate can bet on which debater they believe will win the debate and win in different categories of the debate discussion. The general public can also bet on which audience members they believe will be a part of the top "N" audience members they believe will have the highest truthfulness and fairness scores. Audience members can also win based on certain categories of judging truthfulness and fairness for the top "N" audience winners. These criteria are set by debate producers and promoters.

Ticket sales from the stadium alone are already approaching $450 million, and this does not include sales from advertisements and other promotions. A portion of the event proceeds will go to the winning debater's campaign and the winning "N" audience participants. Some audience members will be physically present at the debate event, while others will participate via Zoom/Teams from their phones, tablets or computers anywhere in the world. Those wanting to participate as an audience judge who are not physically at the event will have to pay $20–$80 to participate online as a voting audience member. With online ticket sales, advertisements and promotions, the event is expected to generate $1.2 billion in sales. The majority of funds will be *used to support worthy social and economic causes previously agreed to by producers and promoters of the event.*

••

ICU debate preparation

ICU More Perfect Union Debates (ICU-MPUD) are a totally different animal. In reality and in the context of this book you can really think of ICU-MPUD as a new form of public protest, WHO summons God into the arena for the purpose of holding protesters and society *__accountable__* for harnessing the deep seated and hardened heart polarization on both sides of the protest as golden nuggets from heaven for redemptively creating the best, More Perfect Union, Win – Win solution for both protesters and society.

Remember my "want to be Nobel prize winning idea" (LOL), opposites in the universe are naturally set up to attract to one another for the purpose of harnessing their differences as the very means for moving to a lower, more stable, more efficient and more perfect energy state or solution. However, what we also discovered was that an object that is still, not moving or at rest will not move, will remain still and will remain at rest, until something outside of itself or maybe inside of itself, creates a force to move the object so that it can move and have the opportunity to be attracted to its opposite. In the context of ICU-MPUD, the first mover, the force, the enzyme that creates the force which summons God into the arena allowing the natural opposing, opposites to attract are the protesters themselves.

ICU-MPUD summon God to the debate arena, using protesters harshest and most toxic debate pain points, to redemptively draw protesters together, by incentivizing protestors to structure and create their protest messages through the eyes of their opposition for the purpose of creating an outcome that exceeds both sides wildest expectations. What da . . .? Wait a minute. Did we say that this is a debate? What the hell is going on here?

Yeah, that's right. Like I told you ICU-MPUD is a totally different animal. ICU-MPUD is a debate event, but this type of debate process actually results in a protest whose purpose is to actually hold protesters and society accountable for bringing resolution and Win – Win More Perfect Union solutions to the protest itself and society at large.

HOW????????

ICU-MPUD were created for the purpose of sponsoring protests, where the polarization between groups on both sides of the protest issue is extreme, toxic and an unbearable pain point plaquing both the protesters and society at large. (Isreal/Hamas War, Abortion, Immigration, Inflation, LGBTQ, etc.). Protests or issues where the differences or polarization between the groups are marginal or only slightly different, ICU-MPUD do not add much value to those type of protest events (Shade of Blue to use on the American flag, Date and Time of President Annual State of the Union Address, etc.)

ICU-MPUD protesters or debate participants include:

1. Debater or a team of debaters representing each side of the issue

2. Proactive online, real-time, audience of debater judges: 10 to 50,000 people

3. Debate/Protest facilitator who summons and keeps God in the Debate-Protest Process

4. Debate/Protest real time scoring and reporting team

5. The general public would be able to observe debate via the ability to broadcast these debates on social media or traditional media outlets when desired

Debater or a team of debaters representing each side of the issue

1. Debater or Debate Team representing a particular side of the issue, win the debate by getting the most points from the online judges for demonstrating Leadership, Empathy, Truth and Creativity by structuring and creating arguments— *through your opponent's eyes*—that creates the best win-win, more perfect unity, between both sides, for the questions being asked.

2. Winning Debater or Winning Debate Team will receive recognition, award, prize etc. Opposition debater or Opposition team will also receive recognition, award, prize, etc.

3. Open book preparation and actual event process. All debate topics and questions will be given to debaters several weeks prior to the debate/protest. Debaters can use any and all resources available to them to prepare for debate topics and questions. All of these resources may be used by debaters during the debate/protest event. No limitations on what debater can use when answering questions during the debate. Debater can read answer or portions of their answer, but debater must remember they are being judged by the opposition who is listening to them and the audience of judges who are listening to and judging them. It's not just what you say. It's also how you say it, when you say it and your non-verbal

communication authenticity that dramatically affects your message and how it is received.

Proactive online, real-time, audience of debater judges: 10 to 50,000 people

1. Audience of Debater judges will be selected directly from a population of protesters on both sides of the issue. As few as ten or as many as 50,000 online judges can participate in the debate.

2. Judges will evaluate each debater argument using four evaluation criteria: Leadership, Creativity, Empathy and Truth, assigning a value of excellent, good, fair, poor, failure for each evaluation criteria for each argument given

3. Audience Judges are an active and very vital part of the debate/protest process. Audience Judges can also be winners in the debate. Audience Judges are evaluate each time they score a debaters argument, to see how fairly they scored debater's argument. Judges with the best cumulative fairness scores, will also be winners in the debate. Audience Judges with the top "N" scores will be winners of the debate with recognition, award and prizes for achieving these levels of performance in the debate.

4. Each Audience Judge will also receive all the topics and all the questions that will be asked in the debate/protest, at the same time that the debaters receives them, several weeks before the event. Audience should study topics and questions and be well prepared for understanding the context under which they are evaluating each debaters arguments as it relates to the four judging evaluation criteria discussed in step 2 above

5. Audience judges, must be courageous and have a gracious heart to serve as an Audience Judge in a ICU-MPUD. Other Audience Judges and the observing public from anywhere around the world will be able to see how you are voting and for who, over the course of the entire debate and what types of fairness scores you are receiving for every evaluation score you assign to each debaters response to questions.

6. At strategic points in the debate, Audience members with the highest fairness score in the debate will be invited to join the on-screen participants and have the opportunity to ask debaters questions and give them their advice or opinions.

7. Audience judges used phones, computers or tablets online to submit their evaluation scores.

Debate/Protest facilitator who summons and keeps God in the Debate-Protest Process

1. Acts as host and facilitator for debate/protest event.

2. Sets tone and atmosphere for the debate/protest

3. Summons and keeps God in the debate and protest by encouraging both debaters and audience judges to both treat themselves and treat other debate/protest participants the same way that they care for, love, protect and develop their own children or loved ones

4. Ask debater, debate questions and instructs/reminds Audience judges on when to evaluate debaters arguments and how to evaluate and score debaters arguments

5. Runs and manages debate/protest event program event

Debate/Protest real time scoring and reporting team

1. Displays topic and questions posed to debater on the screen for viewing audience to see

2. Shows debater scores from Audience judges and who is leading score wise in the debate

3. Shows who are the "N" top Audience judges with the best fairness scores leading the debate in rank order

4. Will show which debater and which Audience Judge is leading in various categories

5. Will show individual Audience Judge scores of debaters, compared to other judges

6. Will be responsible for cutting mikes on or off when speakers have reached time limit

7. Will bring Audience Judges onto the screen and into the conversation at appropriate times during the debate

8. Ability to demonstrate which debater or which Audience Judges were leading the debate at different points in time over the course of the debate. Who was winning when the debate just started, 20% into the debate, 40%, 80%, etc.

Observing public via social media, traditional media, etc., unlimited number of people

1. Observe event

2. Send in comments, recommendations

3. Invite their family, friends and networks to watch and comment, recommendation

4. General public can have access to all the debate topics and all the debate questions at the same time that debaters and Audience judges receive this material. Information all fits on one side of one sheet of paper.

At least 2–4 weeks prior to the event, all participant, debaters, audience, etc. receive all debate topics, questions, rules and complete a survey expressing their preferences on debaters, debate/protest topic issues, etc. A 5–10-minute instruction video will also be available for review. Customer service representatives will be available daily during normal business hours for additional information related to the debate

Debaters record a 1–2-minute video describing who they are and what their views are on the main topics of the debate and why. These two-minute videos will be used by event producers/promoters to market the event in the weeks leading up to the event. Commercials, live events, interviews with debaters and/or audience members discussing the event, anticipating what will be said, what will be argued, who will likely win, why or why not, how this will affect candidate electability, etc. will be widely available in the run-up to the debate.

Commentators providing expert opinion on all of this will appear before, during and after the debate event with discussions and predictions on who should debate next and on what topic, who should be part of the audience of judges, and why, etc.

ICU-MPUD debate rules

1. Debaters are required to convince their opponents that their win-win arguments are best for both sides—*arguing through the eyes, views, beliefs, fears and aspirations of their opponents*

using empathy, truth, creativity and leadership to win the Great Win-win for both sides.

2. The ICU-MPUD process must be used to identify the *most significant* problems requiring resolutions.

3. The ICU-MPUD process must be used to argue the best *win-win* solution for *both* sides.

4. At strategic points throughout the debate, audience judges can ask debaters questions and give them recommendations.

5. Audience judging of the debaters' arguments and behaviors hold debaters accountable in real time: "N" audience participants with the highest fairness scores also win in the debate.

6. Debate facilitators empower debate participants—debaters and judges—to use empathy, truth, creativity and leadership to create the best win-win for all debate participants.

7. Debate winners (both debaters and audience participants) will receive recognition and financial awards agreed upon by producers and promoters of the debate.

8. Ultimately the real winners of the debate will be the public and the debaters who show to the public through their demonstrated behavior what leadership, creativity, truth and empathy looks like in real time and in real life.

9. Who can demonstrate this best with their words, behavior, passion, care, solutions and sincerity? The winner of the ICU-MPUD, that's who! The debater who does this best in the public's eye and is remembered by the public because of their performance and what solutions that they came up with that resonated with the observing public will really be the winner of the debate whether they won by points or not. This is the

real reason and purpose of the ICU debates. In most cases the person who wins based on the points received from the judges during the debate is the winner of the debate in the public's eye, but not always. How many times have we seen a great prize fight that the judges give to one fighter, but the public who saw the fight believe more what they saw with their own eyes and what they heard with their own ears, who the winner of the fight really was. The same thing can happen in an ICU debate.

••

ICU-MPUD event format

- Welcome

- Housekeeping

- Debater/audience stories

- Debate:

    ### Problem ID

    - 1st quarter

    - Audience intervention

    - 2nd quarter

    - Audience intervention

        – Half Time: Debate review

        – Entertainment

    ### Solution

    - 3rd quarter

- Audience intervention
- 4th quarter
  - Awards presentation
  - Post-debate review

A debate in the format of football or basketball games is perfect for ICU-MPUD. The public is already familiar with this entertainment framework. Another potential debate format style is to use the boxing match format where there might be 10 or 15-round competitions. ICU's highly engaging and super viral-creating conversations and behaviors will take engagements to levels never before seen. The intensely interesting and contagious experiences emanating from ICU debates do not exploit the worst and darkest elements our character, but rather develop and empower the best and highest elements of our souls, spirits, characters and aspirations!

Just think about this now, a protests that truly airs the most sensitive, emotional and factual aspects of the most relevant pain points on both sides of the protest issue, clearly spelled out and made aware of two to four weeks before the protest event so that protest participants and the general public have plenty of time to study or make themselves aware of the most important points on both sides of the issue, so that when the protest event occurs, the protest participants and the public will have had the time to thoroughly prepare and be ready to participate or evaluate about what is going to happen at this event, especially since the protest event, agenda and detailed topics and questions have all been released 2–3 weeks prior to the event occurring, also knowing who all the participants of the protest will be, 2–4 weeks prior to the event starting.

But just like in a major prized fight, before the super bowl or the NBA Championship, you know and have seen all the athletes many times before, you have their stats, you have seen them perform before, under many different circumstances and conditions, you know all the rules to the game, where the contest will be held, etc., etc., but what we don't know is what is actually going to happen when you play the game, when opponents are face to face, in live action, under the pressure of competition, observing behavior and circumstances different from what you expect, how do competitors respond to these challenges. Or what if you get just what you expected or planned for, but begin to feel inadequate or overprepared for that situation, and you do not react or respond in the way that you had so religiously prepared and trained for. Here is where that age-old saying adds such great perspective and truth: "**and this is why we play the game.**" There is nothing like transparent, unconstrained but within the rules, full out competition, for the most important issues, most relevant and competitive participants in the game, on full display, right before the publics eyes, in real time, before, during and after an event.

This is Martin Luther King Jr., Non-Violent, Direct Action, Protest Movements 2.0. Protests that start and end with hope, trust, pain, tragedy and despair - and end with more hope, trust, understanding, inclusion, redemptive win-win solutions which create and recommend a much more perfect union among all protest participants and the general public, as a results of living, experiencing and coming out on the other side of the protest – Yaaaaaaaaaaayuuuuuuugh!!!!!!!

We shall overcome…………someday!!!!!!

We (All Americans) have overcome............today!!!!!!!!!!!!

ICU More Perfect Union Debate

President Biden vs. Former President Trump—presidential debate

Debate topic: Making the US economy work best for all Americans

FIRST HALF

PROBLEM IDENTIFICATION—*What has been the biggest obstacle preventing the US economy from working best for all Americans?*

Problem Statement #1: The cumulative effect of unaccounted-for moral hazards caused by slavery, segregation and discrimination against African-Americans (1619–1965) and the outsourcing of industries and jobs to developing countries against middle and low income Americans (1983–2008)

ROUND 1

A. President Biden's challenge—convince Trump through Trump's eyes why you agree the problem statement prevents the US economy from working best for all Americans (or not).

President Biden—Donald, when I listen to many of your concerns about America, most of them have to do with how unfairly you have been treated and how unfairly many of your followers have been treated. Fairness is a pretty big priority for you especially when the unfairness is caused by bigger and more powerful forces in society or in the economy that the victims are powerless to fight against.

This is what has happened to African-Americans because of slavery, segregation and discrimination and many middle and low income Americans because of job losses caused by industry offshoring to Asia and South America over the last forty years.

The wealth ratio between Blacks and whites in America is almost unchanged since before the civil rights movement until today. In the 1950s the wealth ratio between white and Black families was 1 to 7; today it has only slightly improved to 1 to 6.45. If the average wealth of an African-American family in America is $50,000, then the average wealth of a white family in America is $350,000. That is a huge disadvantage for African-American families who are directly responsible for the enormous wealth America earned in such a short period of time during the first 250 years of our country, providing $25 trillion in slave labor, which perfectly explains America's miraculous wealth spurt over that period. African-Americans justly compensated for their contributions to America's miraculous wealth spurt would more than close the wealth gap between Blacks and whites in America.

The buying power of middle- and lower-income Americans from 1970 to today is down 90%. Corporate America incentivized by aggressive conservative government policy sold off large swathes of American industry and jobs to economies in Asia and South America between 1983–2008, transferring about $40 trillion in wealth from middle- and low-income working families to the wealthiest top 10% of Americans over the last forty years. Middle- and lower-income Americans in the bottom 80% can only afford to buy one tenth or ten percent of what they could buy forty years ago.

The negative financial impact on middle- and low-income Americans families is amplified when you consider middle and lower income families have to work two or three jobs now, with half or less than half the benefits, and must also borrow and approach bankruptcy just to keep up with everyday expenses.

Families in the top 10% do not feel this pain because their wealth and income has increased well over 160% over this period. From their perspective the cost of living actually went down dramatically over this period; life is better than ever for them! But only for them.

Donald, I'm sure you can agree with me that this is unfair and one of the major reasons that the US economy does not work best for all Americans, right?

AUDIENCE POINTS FOR JOE: 30

Top 10 Audience Truthfulness and Fairness Judge Leaders

Rank	1st	2nd	3rd	4th	5th	6th	7th	8th	9th	10th
Names	Gretchen, Holmes	Bob, Ramsey	Darren, Holinsworth	Paul, Tolis	Paris, Flood	Cal, Hawkins	Sarah, Buford	Phylis, Lemons	Bernice, Lewis	Carl, Reed

> **B. Former President Trump's challenge**—convince Biden through Biden's eyes that you understood what he said, and give him your opinion on his statements.

Former President Trump—Joe, I agree with you, it's an awful thing how Blacks and the middle class have gotten screwed in this country and it's not right! That is why I want to Make America Great Again, making it possible for these people to have the best opportunity on the planet to be successful, just like me!

I think what Joe said here is good, but he is just catching up with me. I've been saying this since 2015: the people need a change, a new leader who is not afraid to shake things up, to actually make the economy better for these people. The people need *me*!

AUDIENCE POINTS FOR DONALD: 25

Top 10 Audience Truthfulness and Fairness Judge Leaders

Rank	1st	2nd	3rd	4th	5th	6th	7th	8th	9th	10th
Names	Cal, Hawkins	Thelma, Lassiter	Sally, Piller	Paris, Flood	Bob, Ramsey	Jesse, Stafford	Kyle, Jackson	Dwan, Buford	Dan, Howard	Peter, Savage

C. Former President Trump's challenge—convince Biden through Biden's eyes why you agree the problem statement prevents the US economy from working best for all Americans (or not).

Former President Trump—Joe, I know you are a fair man. But you have to admit, America has already paid its dues for slavery. Many Americans died during the Civil War to end slavery and all of the programs we gave Blacks since the civil rights movement should have made everything equal between Blacks and whites by now, in terms of their opportunities for success in America both economically and socially.

We've already had a Black president, for Christ sakes, what more do they want? Now for the good Americans whose jobs and companies were replaced by Chinese and South American workers/companies over the last fifty years, we still have much more work to do! It's time for America to fight back and stick up for our most loyal citizens, who through no fault of their own lost their jobs, industries, communities and entire ways of living.

America needs a leader, bold enough and strong enough to defend and protect the true Americans who deserve support for their loyalty to this great country of ours. So, yes, for the second half of the problem statement, I totally agree.

AUDIENCE POINTS FOR DONALD: 18

TOTAL: 43

Top 10 Audience Truthfulness and Fairness Judge Leaders

Rank	1st	2nd	3rd	4th	5th	6th	7th	8th	9th	10th
Names	Cal, Hawkins	Thelma, Lassiter	Sally, Piller	Paris, Flood	Bob, Ramsey	Jesse, Stafford	Kyle, Jackson	Dwan, Buford	Dan, Howard	Peter, Savage

D. President Biden's challenge—convince Trump through Trump's eyes that you understood what he said and give him your opinion on his statements.

President Biden—Donald, you believe that America has done more than enough to give African-Americans an equal opportunity to be successful in this country by now, no further assistance is needed. However, for the true and loyal Americans who were negatively impacted by the outsourcing of industry and jobs to developing countries over the past fifty years, these Americans are true victims of the US economy and represent a major problem preventing the economy from working best for all Americans.

Donald, I will repeat, America became the wealthiest and most powerful country on this planet in just 270 years, nothing short of a miracle in world history, made possible on the backs of African-Americans, through slavery, segregation and discrimination. America's massive and sustained wealth and power growth in such a record period of time could not have been achieved without the direct contributions from African slavery for 250 years and segregation and discrimination for another 100.

The most vivid proof that America has not paid its debt to African-American citizens is the undeniable fact that the wealth ratio between whites and African-Americans has barely changed from the start of the civil rights movement in the 1950s until today. African-Americans as a people live in the most impoverished communities, have the lowest educational ratings and have the highest crime and incarceration rates.

These well-known and demonstrated facts and truths are not because African-Americans are inherently inferior intellectually or culturally. African-Americans are not inherently more aggressive or more morally depraved, explaining their high crime and incarceration rates. These issues have nothing to do with African–Americans' innate behavior or the color of their skin. But what does "perfectly" explain these differences, very clearly, very directly, very scientifically and very economically is the difference in treatment and opportunities experienced by Africans in this country and the treatment and opportunities that whites experienced in America. What was the difference? The very clear and only differences Africans experienced was 250 years of slavery, and another 100 of segregation and discrimination following slavery. These differences explain precisely the unfair, unjust, and unaccounted-for inequalities between whites and African-Americans today in wealth, education, crime and incarceration rates which remain to this day.

AUDIENCE POINTS FOR JOE: 30

TOTAL: 60

Top 10 Audience Truthfulness and Fairness Judge Leaders

Rank	1st	2nd	3rd	4th	5th	6th	7th	8th	9th	10th
Names	Phylis, Lemons	Sally, Piller	Mary, Grey	Peaches, Green	Paul, Tolls	Niara, Williams	Cal, Hawkins	Dan, Howard	James, Flowers	Paris, Flood

END OF ROUND 1

••

ROUND 2

A. President Biden's challenge—continue to convince Trump through Trump's eyes why you agree the problem statement prevents the US economy from working best for all Americans (or not).

President Biden—Donald, given your tremendous levels of wealth creation and success in life, I am sure you are aware of and have embraced in your wealth creation and investments strategy the principles of diversification and inclusion. Actually diversification and inclusion is not just a core wealth creation and investment strategy. It is a core strategy for winning in general. The most successful organizations and teams have a well-diversified set of talent and resources to deal with the ever-changing marketplace and ever-changing environment in which they operate. Look at the composition of the best, most profitable sports teams in the world, football, basketball, soccer, etc. The diversity of the types of players, with different strengths and weaknesses, serves to balance and create extraordinary value and synergy within the teams to help them perform at the highest levels through player injuries, sickness, player expulsions, rule violations, competing against teams with different and changing talents, styles, strategies, etc...

The bottom 80% of Americans on the wealth and income scale are not being included, developed and harnessed as valued assets in our economy to the extent that they should be, causing America to miss out on the opportunity to create sustainable and robust value added in the US economy beyond our wildest imaginations.

But this requires DEI (Diversity, Equity and Inclusion) for all of our fellow American citizens, the same way you use DEI to diversify and include assets in your financial portfolio to protect against catastrophic losses and capitalize on tremendously outperforming value added opportunities in your wealth-creating endeavors. You are and call yourself the ultimate businessman, Donald. I think you will agree with me that DEI should be for all of our American citizens, with a focus on the bottom 80%, and especially African-Americans, given their excessively unique contributions and catastrophic sacrifices in helping to create the wealthiest and most powerful country on this planet in the shortest period of time ever.

AUDIENCE POINTS FOR JOE: 30

TOTAL: 90

Top 10 Audience Truthfulness and Fairness Judge Leaders

Rank	1st	2nd	3rd	4th	5th	6th	7th	8th	9th	10th
Names	Darren, Holinsworth	Katie, Kuric	Carl, Reed	Charles, Tungston	Jackie, Gates	Mary, Grey	Gretchen, Holmes	Kristie, Harris	Kylie, Jackson	Sally, Pillar

> **B. Former President Trump's challenge**—convince Biden through Biden's eyes that you understood what he said and give him your opinion on his statements.

Former President Trump—Joe, as you know, I am a man of great wealth, and I truly do like your twist on the Diversity, Equity, and Inclusion principle. It is true that, in general, having a team or portfolio of assets that are well diversified, integrated and synergize so that they are maximally working together to protect my financial and business portfolio under conditions of excessive and even sustained volatility, not only saves the business from catastrophic losses, but creates opportunities to capture unimaginable returns, at the right time and in the right place, precisely because of the synergized mix of diverse assets that are available and have been included in my business and financial assets. Given your financial analogy, Joe, I agree with you, wholeheartedly, on the value of DEI when it is explained in this context: Not bad for an old goat, Joe!

AUDIENCE POINTS FOR DONALD: 45

TOTAL: 88

Top 10 Audience Truthfulness and Fairness Judge Leaders

Rank	1st	2nd	3rd	4th	5th	6th	7th	8th	9th	10th
Names	Jane, Davis	Carl, Reed	Pam, Brown	Sarah, Buford	Gretchen, Holmes	Phylis, Lemons	Karen, Jones	Dan, Howard	Chase, Reese	Kyle, Jackson

C. Former President Trump's challenge—continue to convince Biden through Biden's eyes why *you* agree the problem statement prevents the US economy from working best for all Americans (or not).

Former President Trump—Now Joe, I know you and your people are having a brain fart after hearing me praise you and give you kudos on your DEI analogy. But it's OK, Joe. My base support over the last nine years have been stuck at a constant 43%, year in and year out. I have been looking for something to break me through that barrier, Joe. And DEI repackaged and rebranded the "Make America Great Again" way is just what I've been looking for! So Joe, when you get up off the floor from having your brain fart, because you got me to agree with you, check out the polls a couple of weeks from now, when the Donald Trump DEI Campaign and Recruitment Strategy is in full effect . . . Joe, you old goat, you've given me a gift that will keep on giving . . .

AUDIENCE POINTS FOR DONALD: 35

TOTAL: 123

Top 10 Audience Truthfulness and Fairness Judge Leaders

Rank	1st	2nd	3rd	4th	5th	6th	7th	8th	9th	10th
Names	Justin, Burns	Sally, Piller	Carl, Reed	Charles, Tungston	Mary, Grey	Jane, Davis	Dwan, Buford	Regia, Samson	Paul, Tolls	John, Akers

D. **President Biden's challenge**—convince Trump through Trump's eyes that you understood what he said and give him your opinion on his statements.

President Biden—You know what, Donald, to be frank with you, I'm surprised. I actually thought that you were so blinded by your narcissism that you would not see a gift thrown at you if it smacked you dead in the face. Not sure if I can believe what I've just seen with my eyes and heard with my own ears coming out of your mouth, Donald, but Halleluia, this is good for the America people. We both agree that developing and creating equal opportunity for every American to be the best possible versions of themselves for inclusion and maximum participation in the American economy and American society is the ultimate goal, and will remove one of the biggest obstacles in making the US economy work best for all Americans.

AUDIENCE POINTS FOR JOE: 45

TOTAL: 135

Top 10 Audience Truthfulness and Fairness Judge Leaders

Rank	1st	2nd	3rd	4th	5th	6th	7th	8th	9th	10th
Names	James, Rowers	Kate, Kuric	Niara, Williams	Sarah, Buford	John, Akers	Bernece, Lewis	Phylis, Lemons	Charles, Tungston	Paris, Flood	Peter, Savage

••

Problem Statement #2: Broken and uneconomic, the US economy acts more like a Ponzi Scheme, skewed to work best for the wealthiest top 10% in America, on course to bankrupt all of America in the next five to ten years if the status quo of the last fifty years persists going forward.

Round 1

A. President Biden's challenge—convince Trump through Trump's eyes why you agree the problem statement prevents the US economy from working best for all Americans (or not).
President Biden—Donald, when I listen to…

••

What the . . . What just happened here? Maga Man and Old Joe gradually coming to an agreement on what the underlying problems are in the US economy! Agreement on what the problems are is the fundamental starting point for working together on a good and sustainable solution that actually works best for all Americans. But how did this happen? How did we have two tragically polar opposites get in a debate ring with the fate of their election hopes swinging in the balance and both moving toward an agreement on not just what helps them and their constituents the best but what helps all Americans the best?

That sounds like magic in these days of polarization, envy, strife, hate, and vindictiveness. No, that actually sounds like a miracle! Yes, miracle! ICU (I See You) More Perfect Union debates are a product of the cumulative wisdom and knowledge that has existed since the beginning of time to this day. It is life, saving itself, from itself. I call ICU-MPUD events "God's Arena". Who has the leadership, integrity, creativity and empathy to step into God's arena, naked and exposed and ready to go to combat, putting everything on the line to win the Great Win-win for humankind on this planet?

When I first saw Mixed Martial Arts cage fighting, I was so impressed and said to myself that this form of competitive fighting is the ultimate fighting competition and experience, with the ability to use all parts of your body and any fighting style desired to compete and win. In my mind this is the ultimate competitive environment, no hiding place, no excuses, no place to run… However, ICU (I See You) More Perfect Union debates are on an entirely different level of competition.

In ICU-MPUD, not only are there no places to hide or make excuses, but they require transcendence of the spirit. Opponents are not only maximally prepared and fine-tuned to fight for and represent their own views and those of their constituents, but they must fight for and argue their views from the perspectives, interests, thoughts, emotions, pains, experiences and aspirations of their most adversarial or hated opponents, with the ultimate goal of not destroying their opponent by all means necessary, but rather winning the best win-win possible for both sides as best as is humanly possible. In this context, ICU-MPUD make MMA competitions look like a beautiful walk through the park on a gorgeous sunny day in the spring of the year.

The ICU-MPUD process is like the gestation period prior to birth. The result of the ICU-MPUD, like the result of the human gestation period, is new life which holds the potential for better, greater or the best win-wins that humankind has ever discovered, developed or created. ICU debates when successfully executed are the existential expression of life itself, saving itself, from itself, even though it has an equal opportunity, power and ability to destroy itself.

Regeneration is life's natural process of restoring cells or even entire body parts that have become damaged. ICU on the other hand is a willful act of the life process that is not automatic; it is a choice. It is a first mover choice, like the first mover God made to create the universe. We are made in the image and likeness of God and have that same power through the conscious choices that we make over the course of our lives. ICU-MPUD harness and awaken the consciousness of reality in all of us to help us make Godly decisions which are in our own individual and collective best interest.

Now, let's take a closer look at some of the components of ICU-MPUD and more examples of how they can be used in very different critical areas of society and life in general:

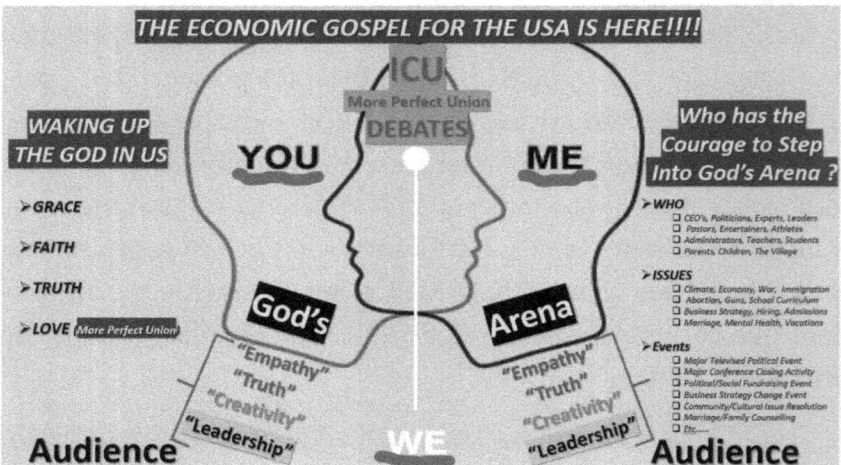

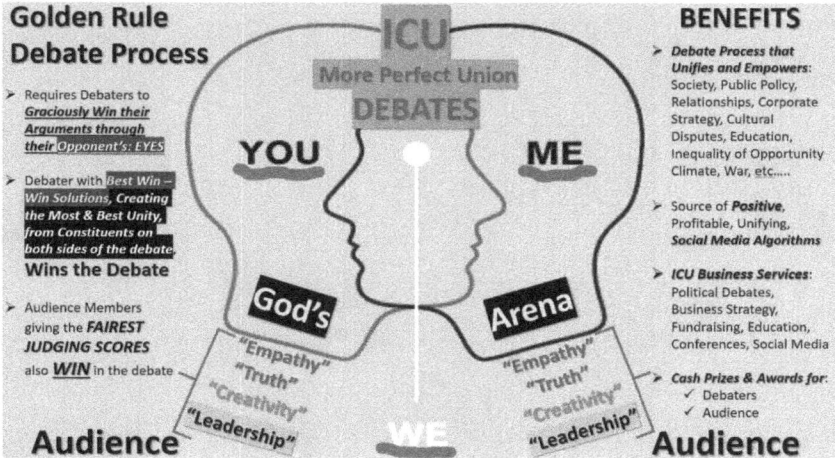

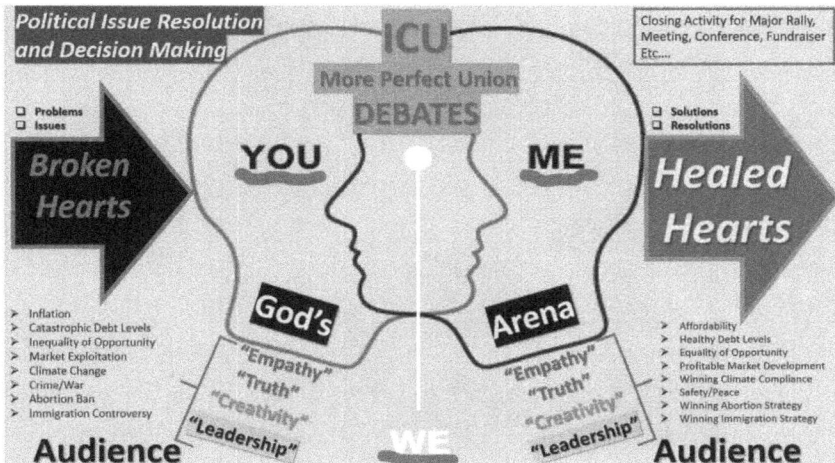

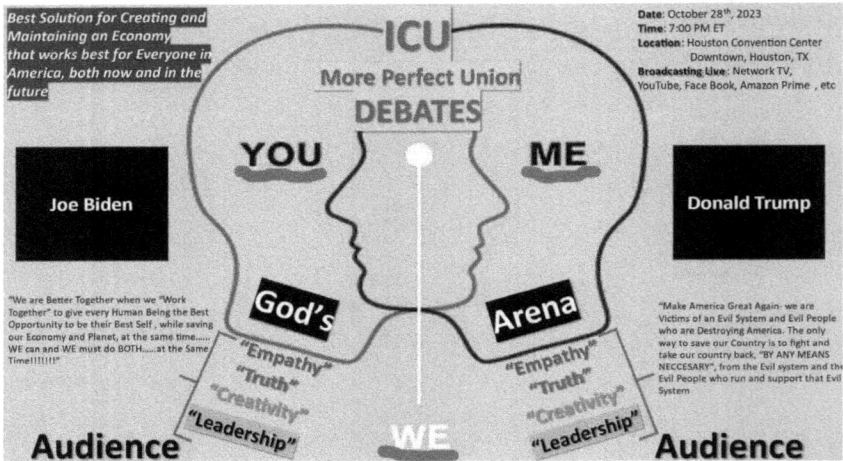

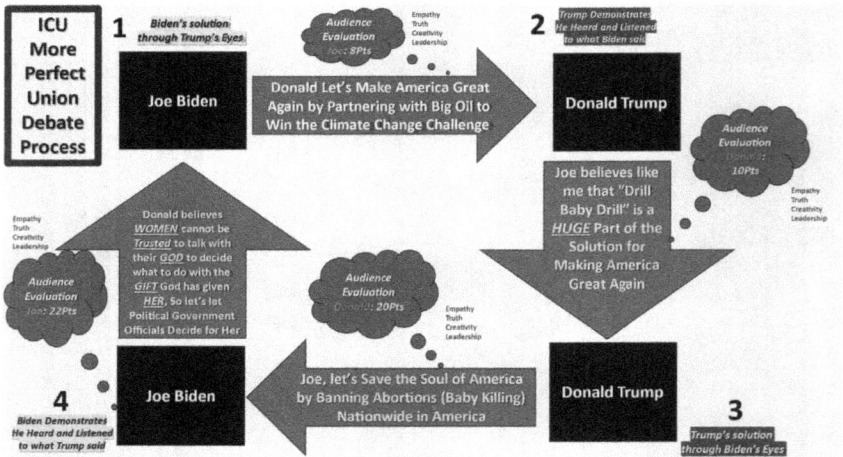

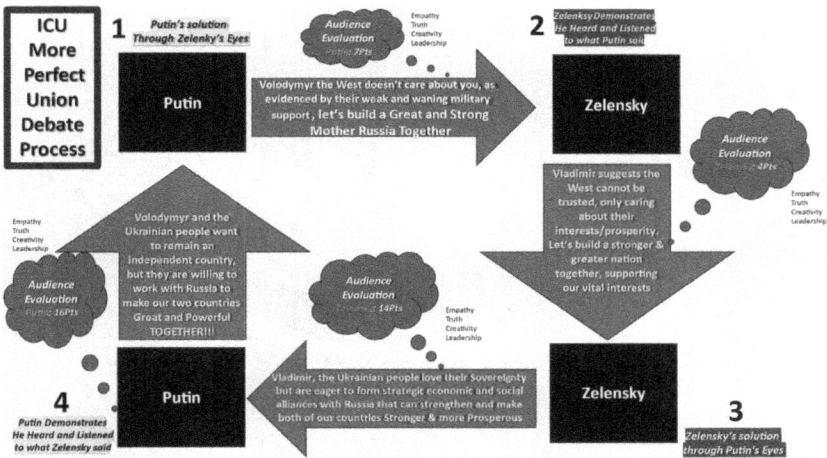

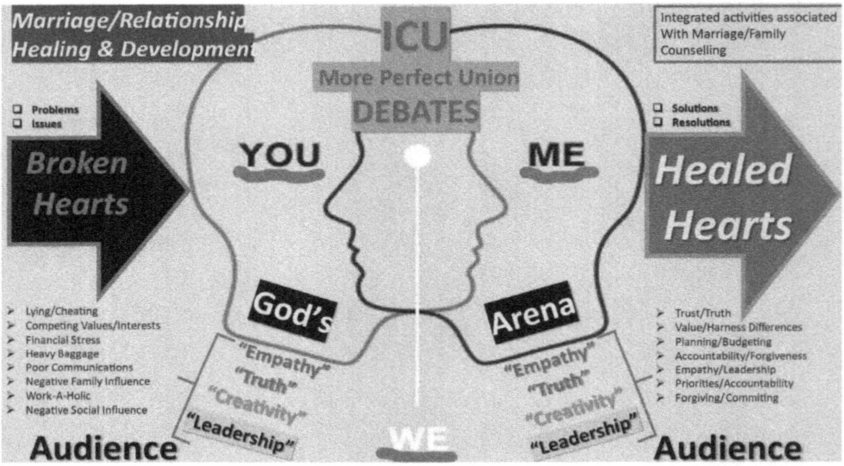
Marriage/Relationship Healing & Development
ICU
More Perfect Union
DEBATES
Integrated activities associated With Marriage/Family Counselling
Problems
Issues
Broken Hearts
YOU
ME
Solutions
Resolutions
Healed Hearts
God's
Arena
Lying/Cheating
Competing Values/Interests
Financial Stress
Heavy Baggage
Poor Communications
Negative Family Influence
Work-A-Holic
Negative Social Influence
"Empathy"
"Truth"
"Creativity"
"Leadership"
Trust/Truth
Value/Harness Differences
Planning/Budgeting
Accountability/Forgiveness
Empathy/Leadership
Priorities/Accountability
Forgiving/Commiting
Audience
WE
Audience

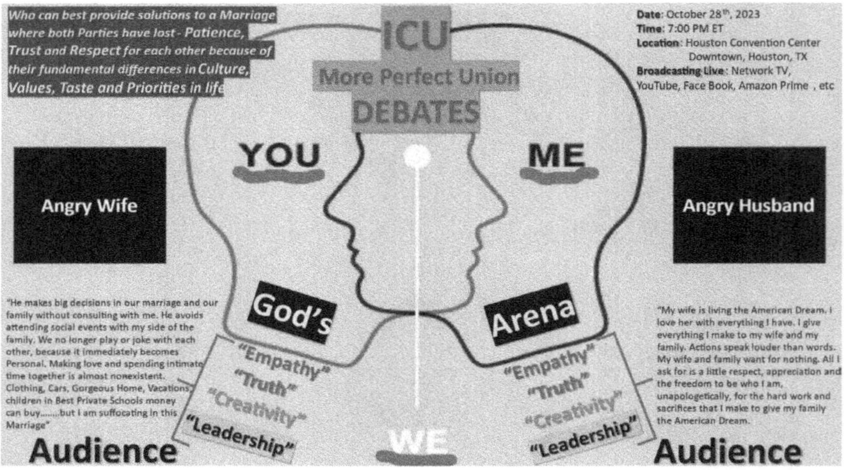
Who can best provide solutions to a Marriage where both Parties have lost - Patience, Trust and Respect for each other because of their fundamental differences in Culture, Values, Taste and Priorities in life
ICU
More Perfect Union
DEBATES
Date: October 28th, 2023
Time: 7:00 PM ET
Location: Houston Convention Center Downtown, Houston, TX
Broadcasting Live: Network TV, YouTube, Face Book, Amazon Prime , etc
YOU
ME
Angry Wife
Angry Husband
God's
Arena
"He makes big decisions in our marriage and our family without consulting with me. He avoids attending social events with my side of the family. We no longer play or joke with each other, because it immediately becomes Personal. Making love and spending intimate time together is almost nonexistent. Clothing, Cars, Gorgeous Home, Vacations, children in Best Private Schools money can buy........but I am suffocating in this Marriage"
"My wife is living the American Dream. I love her with everything I have. I give everything I make to my wife and my family. Actions speak louder than words. My wife and family want for nothing. All I ask for is a little respect, appreciation and the freedom to be who I am, unapologetically, for the hard work and sacrifices that I make to give my family the American Dream.
"Empathy"
"Truth"
"Creativity"
"Leadership"
Audience
WE
Audience

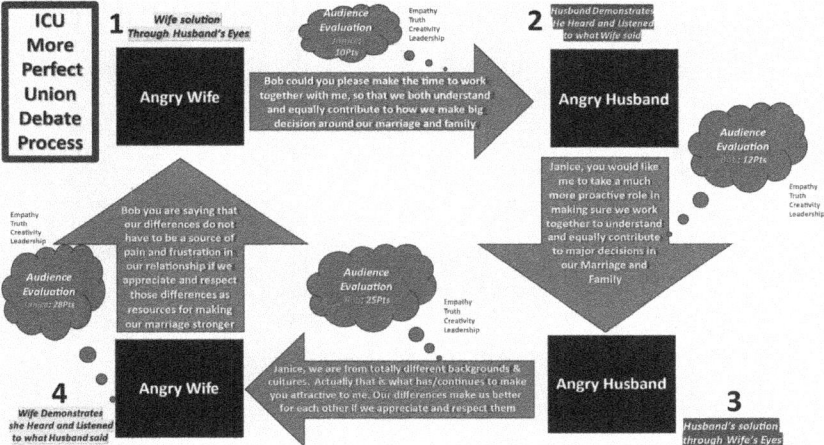

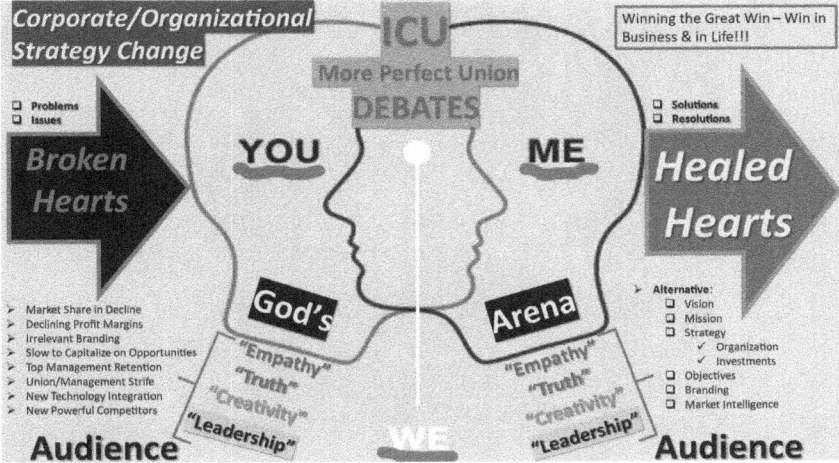

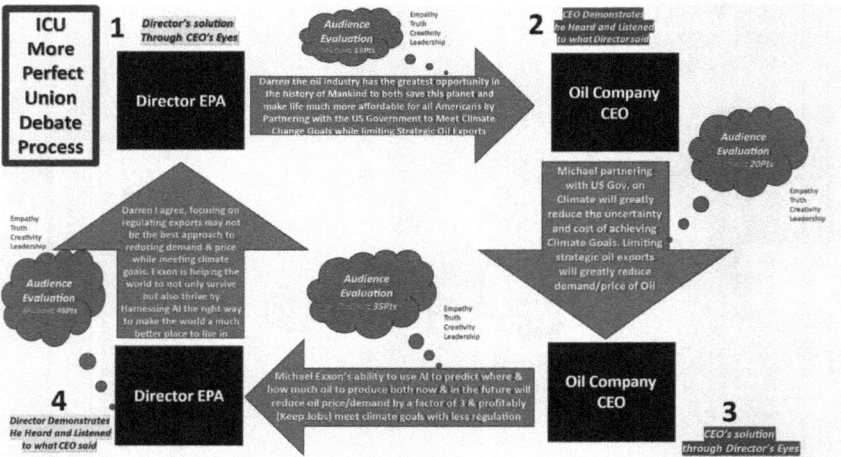

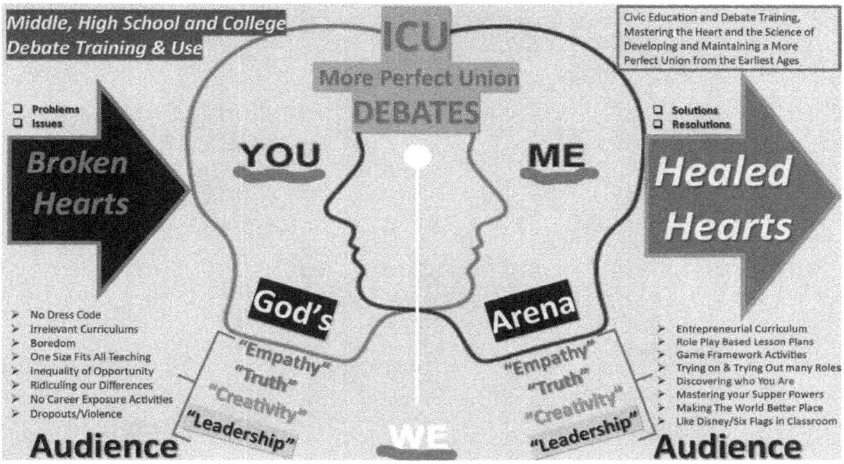
Middle, High School and College
Debate Training & Use
ICU
More Perfect Union
DEBATES
Civic Education and Debate Training, Mastering the Heart and the Science of Developing and Maintaining a More Perfect Union from the Earliest Ages
Problems
Issues
Broken Hearts
Solutions
Resolutions
Healed Hearts
YOU
ME
God's
Arena
No Dress Code
Irrelevant Curriculums
Boredom
One Size Fits All Teaching
Inequality of Opportunity
Ridiculing our Differences
No Career Exposure Activities
Dropouts/Violence
"Empathy"
"Truth"
"Creativity"
"Leadership"
Entrepreneurial Curriculum
Role Play Based Lesson Plans
Game Framework Activities
Trying on & Trying Out many Roles
Discovering who You Are
Mastering your Supper Powers
Making The World Better Place
Like Disney/Six Flags in Classroom
Audience
WE
Audience

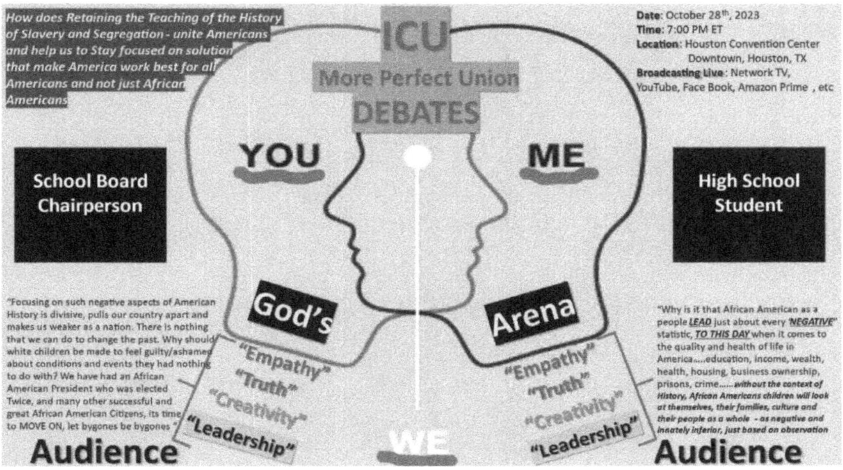
How does Retaining the Teaching of the History of Slavery and Segregation - unite Americans and help us to Stay focused on solution that make America work best for all Americans and not just African Americans
ICU
More Perfect Union
DEBATES
Date: October 28th, 2023
Time: 7:00 PM ET
Location: Houston Convention Center Downtown, Houston, TX
Broadcasting Live: Network TV, YouTube, Face Book, Amazon Prime , etc
YOU
ME
School Board Chairperson
High School Student
God's
Arena
"Focusing on such negative aspects of American History is divisive, pulls our country apart and makes us weaker as a nation. There is nothing that we can do to change the past. Why should white children be made to feel guilty/ashamed about conditions and events they had nothing to do with? We have had an African American President who was elected Twice, and many other successful and great African American Citizens, its time to MOVE ON, let bygones be bygones "
"Empathy"
"Truth"
"Creativity"
"Leadership"
"Why is it that African American as a people LEAD just about every 'NEGATIVE" statistic, TO THIS DAY when it comes to the quality and health of life in America.....education, income, wealth, health, housing, business ownership, prisons, crime......without the context of History, African Americans children will look at themselves, their families, culture and their people as a whole - as negative and innately inferior, just based on observation
Audience
WE
Audience

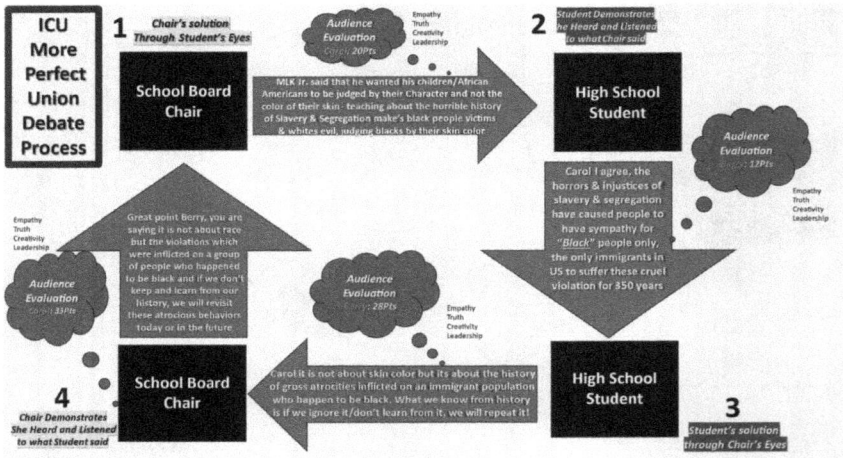

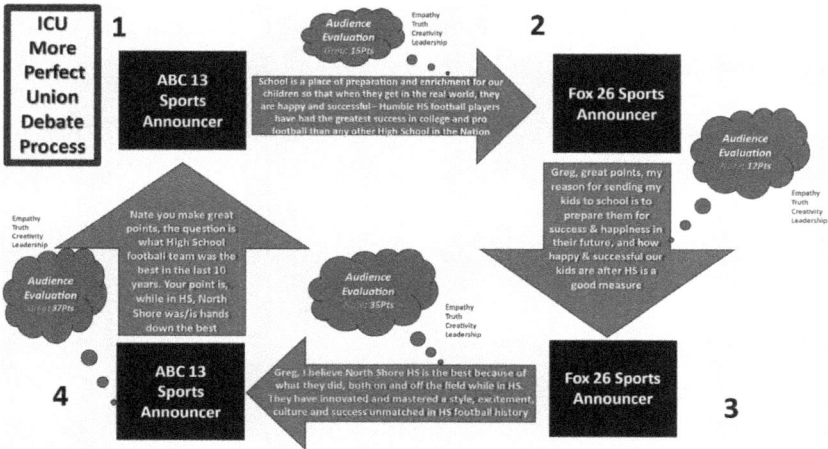

ICU (I See You) More Perfect Union debates are much more than a nice, new way to debate and discuss ideas around contentious topics and issues in life. ICU debates are a moral and just means for helping Americans to fall in love with being American again. At their core, ICU debates are the very essence of the US Constitution incarnate. They take on the toughest, most complex and most polarizing issues and problems confronting mankind today in a way that:

- Heals the broken-hearted
- Brings sight to the blind
- Sets the captives free

The more polarizing and complex the problems or issues under consideration are, the more applicable the ICU debate process is for solving or bringing a resolution to these problems or issues. There is an old saying, "There is no problem that is too big for God to handle or solve." ICU (I See You) More Perfect Union debates are God's Arena. "Who dares enter God's Arena and help the human race, morally and justly, save itself from itself, for itself and future generations?"

ICU (I See You) More Perfect Union debates—coming to a platform available to you very soon.

LET'S DO THIS!

www.ingramcontent.com/pod-product-compliance
Lightning Source LLC
Chambersburg PA
CBHW032104280326
41933CB00009B/759